TATE

SUG

Something for the Girls

Something for the Girls

The Official Guide to the First 100 Years of Guiding

Alison Maloney

Foreword by HM The Queen

www.girlguiding.org.uk

To the generations of volunteers who have made guiding happen

Constable & Robinson

3 The Lanchesters

162 Fulham Palace Road

London W6 9ER

www.constablerobinson.com

First published in the UK in 2009 by Constable,

an imprint of Constable & Robinson Ltd

ISBN: 978-1-84529-780-0

1 3 5 7 9 10 8 6 4 2

Design by Itonic Design Ltd, Brighton

Contents

ABOVE: SRS
Duke of York
Rangers Princess
Margaret and
Princess Elizabeth
peel potatoes with
their unit on board
MTB 630

Foreword

SANDRINGHAM HOUSE

The lives of millions of girls and women around the world have been influenced by the Girl Guide Movement during the first 100 years of its remarkable history.

My own long and close association with guiding began in 1937 when Princess Margaret and I enrolled – she as a Brownie and I as a Guide. I have fond memories of my years as a Sea Ranger, and of becoming Chief Ranger of the British Empire and then Patron of the Guide Association. Princess Margaret was to become President, a role that she pursued with warm commitment for over 30 years.

While the core values of guiding have remained constant, I have been delighted to watch it evolve, led by the ambitions and needs of the girls of the day. The pages of this book chart that story of change, describing the challenge and the advancement coupled with the fun and adventure that is guiding. Every chapter tells of the dedication of the volunteers of yesterday and today who have given so much of their time and of themselves. My good wishes to each one of them as they celebrate 100 years of guiding.

I send my warmest congratulations to Girlguiding UK on the occasion of its Centenary as it continues to reach out to new communities and give more girls the space they need to grow in confidence.

ELIZABETH R.

29th January 2009.

Introduction

What you have in your hands now is a celebration of the past, the present and the future. But the chronology in the book ends there: it is not arranged from 1909 through the decades, as might be expected. Instead, the fascinating story of guiding is told through four themes which are, were and always will be the very essence of the movement.

We are proud that the themes of being inclusive, giving girls a voice, providing girl-only activities and being modern and relevant were all there in 1909 when a group of young girls dared to 'gatecrash' the Scout rally at Crystal Palace, and lobby Robert Baden-Powell to provide 'something for the girls'. This book starts from that historic moment – for he listened to their case and the results of their action went on to reverberate around the globe.

The first section of the book highlights how guiding has always been diverse and inclusive. Members in the early days cut across the Edwardian class system, as they included factory girls as well as the better-off. The movement spread across the world, and today there are more than 10 million girls involved. In the UK, inclusivity takes many forms, from groups thriving in inner cities and deprived areas to clever adaptation by Leaders to include disabled members in their unit activities.

The second section, 'A Guiding Voice', gives some wonderful examples of how guiding has given girls a platform for their views. The common factor here is girls making a statement, either vocally or through high-profile actions. This happened in various ways depending on the point in history, but they were always topical, groundbreaking and inspiring. Today the advancement of women is just as much a theme as it was in 1909 and many women in prominent roles today count the skills they learned in guiding among their most important training for their careers – and speaking out is always one of them!

'Girl Power', the third section, emphasises the 'girl-only space' that is guiding. Here you will find examples of the amazing variety of activities and more extreme challenges that build girls' self-confidence in a safe, friendly, relaxed environment. From the first time a seven-year-old Brownie stays at an overnight camp through to a two-week trek to Everest for over-18s, age-appropriate confidence-building challenges have always been part of the guiding experience.

The final section contains many illustrations of how guiding has everything for the modern girl. Today's programme of activities and badges would hardly be recognised by the pioneering young women who started the movement – but they would certainly recognise its spirit. That spirit includes personal growth achieved through learning and community action on both a local and a global scale. Most of all, it is about the absolute confidence that guiding will continue to evolve, to remain contemporary and compelling for the girls and young women of the future.

So, the message of this book says loud and clear: at our Centenary, this is guiding today. Our first hundred years have shaped our present and this heritage will continue to shape our future.

1

Something for Everyone

The Beginnings

In 1909, in a world where men wore the trousers and women had no vote, the actions of a few feisty girls were to lead to the establishment of the world's largest organisation for girls and young women, a movement that was to transcend the barriers of background, race, nationality and faith. One hundred years on, more than half a million girls in the UK and 10 million across the globe continue to push boundaries, following the example of the generations of guides who have gone before them. Their story is the story of 100 years of girls in the lead.

An angry exchange in the *Spectator* in December 1909 showed how strongly opposed many adults were to the thought of the Scout movement, then still in its infancy, being infiltrated by girls. Violet R. Markham, for example, declared, 'Girls are not boys, and the training which

RIGHT: Girls at the Crystal Palace Rally in 1909. From the *Illustrated London News*

THE FIRST RALLY

SOME OF THE GIRL SCOUTS AT THE CRYSTAL PALACE LAST SATURDAY
The Scout idea has spread to girls, of whom forty (mostly from Shoreditch and Reigate) were present at the great review at the Crystal Palace last Saturday. The King sent a message to the Boy Scouts: "Please assure the boys that the King takes the greatest interest in them, and tell them that if he should call upon them later in life, the sense of patriotic responsibility and habits of discipline which they are now acquiring as boys will enable them to do their duty as men should any danger threaten the Empire."

No. 183

Boy Scouts

Crystal Palace.

Sept. 4, 1909.

First ❊ Rally

Complimentary

develops manly qualities in one, may lead to the negation of womanliness in the other.' The editor of the magazine heartily agreed, urging Robert Baden-Powell to 'stop this mischievous new development.' Another letter-writer added: 'I cannot conceive that any thoughtful parent can doubt that in any circumstances whatsoever, this is a foolish and pernicious movement.'

The roots of this heated discussion lay in an event two months earlier, on 4 September, when Robert Baden-Powell held the first Scout Rally at the Crystal Palace. Despite the miserable, cold and wet weather, 11,000 Scouts turned up and 'The Chief' got a bit of a surprise: among the thousands of lads was a handful of 'Girl Scouts' who represented many more from all over the country. These determined girls were dressed in a variation of the Scout uniform with a fleur-de-lis on their hats, and were carrying poles and haversacks.

RIGHT: 1912 Guide
with biplane

BOTH PAGES:
Some early
badges, including
the red Nursing
Sister badge,
Electrician, Flyer
and Sportswoman

when Baden-Powell approached another small group of girls and asked 'Who are you?', the reply was 'We're Girl Scouts'. His reply to that was 'You can't be; there aren't any Girl Scouts'.

Three girls came from Pinkneys Green in Berkshire, which was later to become the first Girl Guide Company registered and Agnes Baden-Powell's Own. Two girls selected to represent the Girls Emergency Corps brought up the rear of the parade as a special privilege. Sybil Cannadine was among eight girls from Camberwell and Peckham in South London, and Nesta Maude and Rotha Orman travelled from Forest Mere in Hampshire.

Back came their answer: 'Oh yes there are, 'cos we're them!' Baden-Powell replied, 'That's impossible, this is only for boys.' The girls pleaded for 'something for the girls please', to which he answered 'I'll think about it'.

Marguerite De Beaumont led one of the earliest Girls Scout Patrols, the Wolves from North London. When Baden-Powell asked, 'Who are you and what are you doing here?' she answered, 'Please Sir, we are the Wolf Patrol of the Girl Scouts, and we want to do Scouting like the boys.'

Years later, when asked who started the Girl Guide movement, his reply was 'They started themselves when they first attended the Crystal Palace Rally'.

There were also a few unattached and other sizeable detachments of girls. (One newspaper spoke of 40 girls attending, mostly from Shoreditch and Reigate.) The two girls from Forest Mere later wrote about joining 15 other girls at the Rally and wishing they had the right to join the boys in the march past. It was also reported that

Certainly the seed of an idea was planted then: a pamphlet from 1910 says, 'Some 6,000 girls have registered themselves.' From his army days, Baden-Powell recalled an Indian regiment called the Khyber Guides who had impressed him with their discipline and bravery, so he decided that Guides would be an apt name for these pioneering young women. Setting up an entirely new movement, separate from the Scouts, and persuading its members to accept the title Girl Guides, went some way to calming the fears of those Scouts who opposed the presence of girls. But, in an age when girls wore ankle-length skirts and physical exercise was frowned upon, the idea met with a huge amount of opposition.

In 1910 Baden-Powell asked his sister Agnes to organise and lead the new movement; she readily agreed. To appease critics, the first two pamphlets produced on the Girl Guide Association included a letter from a mother in India to her child who was being educated in England. She protested at her daughter's involvement in Scouting:

What you say about Scouting having helped you have more self-control is, of course, all to the good, but why WHISTLE to work off your feelings? You do not want to have a man's mouth, I suppose, with big strong lips and perhaps a moustache (!); you would not BE a man even then. Do you know that there are more girls nowadays with hairy lips than formerly, and I believe it is due to the violent exercise they take, and romping it generally – it's no joke.

The concerned parent went on to suggest that if Scouting for girls was to 'produce lovable, splendid WOMEN, it must be on its own lines, and certain things must be given up and others cultivated'.

Having printed the letter, Agnes Baden-Powell used the sentiments to distance her Guides from the Scouts. 'The mother's objections to Scouting,' she wrote, 'with which I cordially agree, will, I hope, be met by the institution of Girl Guides.'

Early Girl Guides practised first aid, signalling, drill and stretcher work, and their badges included Cook, Sailor, Tailor and Clerk. By the end of 1910, there were 22 badges, including Telegraphist and Electrician. The advent of the First World War gave the girls an opportunity to prove the usefulness of the skills they had learned and silenced many critics. From then on the movement continued to grow until today, 100 years later, its members come from some 145 countries across the world.

BELOW: The Guide Law, written in hand by Robert Baden-Powell, which now hangs at Foxlease

This is
The Guide Law

I.   A Guide's Honour is to be Trusted

II.   A Guide is Loyal to her King and her Guiders, her parents, her country and her employers or employees

III. A Guide's Duty is to be useful and to help others

IV.   A Guide is a friend to all and a sister to every other Guide no matter to what social class she belongs.

V.   A Guide is courteous

VI.   A Guide is a friend to animals

VII. A Guide obeys orders : of her parents, patrol leader, or captain without question

VIII. A Guide smiles and sings under all difficulties

IX.   A Guide is Thrifty

X.   A Guide is pure in thought, word, and deed

XI.   · · · · · · [This law is unwritten but is understood]

A Guide is not a Fool

Baden-Powell of Gilwell
Founder.

Lord Baden-Powell

1857–1941

Though Robert Baden-Powell was born in London, it was in the country that the adventurous spirit and practical skills that were to shape his life came to the fore. At Charterhouse school in Surrey, the young Baden-Powell made the surrounding woods his own, stalking his masters and catching and cooking rabbits, always making sure the smoke from his fire didn't give him away. During the holidays one year he and his brothers went on a yachting expedition around the south coast of England and on another they traced the River Thames to its source by canoe.

It was towards the end of his outstanding military career (which in 1909 led to his knighthood), that his ideas for scouting crystallised. During the siege of Mafeking, in South Africa, he was so impressed by the skills and resourcefulness of the young boys he used as 'scouts' that he set about writing *Aids to Scouting*. In 1907 he took 22 boys from all walks of life to Brownsea Island, to try out his plans. This first Scout camp was a roaring success and was followed a year later by his famous book *Scouting for Boys* – which of course was also read by a substantial number of girls.

On the advice of King Edward VII, who suggested he could serve his country more effectively through the Scout movement than he could as a soldier, in 1910 Baden-Powell retired from the army. He then asked his sister Agnes to form the Girl Guide movement, following the success of the Crystal Palace Rally in 1909. The movement was boosted further with his marriage to Olave Soames, who took up the cause with energy and enthusiasm.

The 1921 New Year's honours list created a baronetcy for Baden-Powell, who became Lord Baden-Powell of Gilwell in 1928, after the international training centre for Scout Leaders. In 1938 he and Olave relocated to Nyeri, Kenya, where he died on 8 January 1941. His headstone reads 'Robert Baden-Powell, Chief Scout of the World', under the badges of the Scouts and Guides.

**RIGHT:
Robert
Baden-Powell
in 1896**

BELOW: The Chief Guide and the Chief Scout in 1932

A Girl's World

RIGHT: Girl Scouts in Japan

Within a year of the birth of guiding in the UK, units sprang up in Canada, Denmark, Finland, New Zealand, Poland, South Africa and Sweden, and, a year after that in Australia, Ireland, the Netherlands and India, which at that time included Bangladesh and Pakistan. Five more countries, including the US, Norway and Zimbabwe, established troops in 1912, and by 1930 another 15 countries, including Brazil, China and Estonia, joined the fold. Each country adopted its own uniform, badges and rules, but they were all based on the principles originally set out by Robert Baden-Powell in 1910.

In April 1914 Agnes Baden-Powell welcomed the first overseas Guides to visit Great Britain. Guides in the UK were glad to meet their German counterparts at a party at University Hall in London, unaware that the two countries would be at war just four months later.

The original WAGGGS

In 1919 the Imperial Council was founded by Olave Baden-Powell to promote and maintain contact between Girl Guides and Girl Scouts around the globe.

WAGGGS' mission

To enable girls and young women to develop their fullest potential as responsible citizens of the world.

WAGGGS' vision for 2011

We are a growing worldwide movement – the voice of girls and young women who influence issues they care about and aim to build a better world.

A year later the first International Conference was held in Oxford, where the Chief Guide told the attendants: 'We have not met to organise and argue; we have come together as a big happy family to exchange thoughts and to get to know each other and learn from each other and we hope from this gathering we shall go away filled with greater knowledge and greater keenness and inspired to go forward with our work for our sisterhood.'

A total of 24 countries was represented, though some struggled for acceptance. In Romania, for example, the Guide movement had degenerated into an athletic society and had not survived the war years, while in Russia politics had crept in: it had two separate factions, one Bolshevik and the other anti-Bolshevik.

There was good news too, with Japan reporting encouragement from parents and children who are 'keen, well-behaved and intelligent', and a Polish representative speaking glowingly of the Guides' inspiring work throughout the grim war years. At the time of the conference there were 183,533 members in the UK, 25,815 in British territories and 112,185 elsewhere.

TOP AND BOTTOM: Girl Scouts from the Philippines and Guides from Japan at the World Camp in Foxlease, 1999

Founder of WAGGGS members:

Australia
Belgium
Canada
Czechoslovakia
Denmark
Estonia
Finland
France
Hungary
Iceland
India
Japan
Latvia
Liberia
Lithuania
Luxembourg
The Netherlands
New Zealand
Norway
Poland
South Africa
Sweden
Switzerland
The United Kingdom
and Northern Ireland
The United States
Yugoslavia

The conferences continued every two years until, in 1926, after the fourth was held in the US, representatives suggested forming an association. 'A big step for the Movement was taken when at the International Conference in Budapest, a World Bureau was formed,' wrote Robert Baden-Powell in 1928. 'It was placed under the direction of Dame Katherine Furse and is very much on the lines of that which is working so successfully for the Boy Scouts. It has brought our whole sisterhood into definite touch and solidarity on a good foundation for facing wonderful possibilities in the direction of world amity and peace.'

The delegates at the Fifth International Conference discussed the idea of an umbrella organisation bringing together the 26 countries with a significant Guide presence. The result was The World Association of Girl Guides and Girl Scouts (WAGGGS), set up in 1928 and ratified two years later at Foxlease in Hampshire, where a flag, designed by Norwegian Frøken Kari Aas, was also approved.

Today, WAGGGS provides girls with an opportunity to learn more about their peers in other countries, to meet fellow guiding members from other countries and to do their bit to change the world. Working together with global bodies such as the United Nations (UN), UNICEF and the World Health Organisation (WHO), the girls take part in a huge variety of projects to provide aid, water and sanitation in developing countries as well as helping to combat the spread of sexual infections and teenage pregnancies.

For over 60 years voluntary teams working with the UN have been based in Geneva, Nairobi, New York, Paris, Rome and Vienna. Among their projects is the introduction of the AIDS badge, to promote understanding and awareness of HIV and AIDS among young women. Since 1967 members have also run a Mutual Aid Scheme, whereby associations in developed countries pledge money to buy equipment, train leaders and contribute to important projects run by associations in poorer regions.

In recent years, WAGGGS has also teamed up with WHO in a campaign to prevent adolescent pregnancy as well as launching projects linked to Global Action Days such as No Drugs Day, World Water Day, World Peace Day and 2007's Walk the World Day.

Many members added their names to UNIFEM'S Internet campaign, 'Say NO to violence against women'. Actress Nicole Kidman added her voice to the campaign, saying 'For International Women's Day 2008, I would like to invite all Girl Guides and Girl Scouts to help me speak out.' Over a million names were delivered to the UN Secretary General, Ban Ki-moon.

In 2009 WAGGGS introduced its Global Action Theme and encouraged girls worldwide to say 'together we can change our world'.

ABOVE: The World Badge can be worn by members of any Guide Association belonging to WAGGGS. It was adopted in 1947, at the 11th World Conference in France, and was followed in 1950 by a World Brownie Badge

FAR LEFT: The Baden-Powells at the Fifth World Conference, held in Hungary in 1928

LEFT: Girls at World Camp

RIGHT: Washing-up stand at the World Camp, 1924

LEFT: At the World Camp in 1924, Robert Baden-Powell signs autographs for French Guides

RIGHT: The Transport Section has dinner

World camps

The Centenary year will see 2,000 international members joining 5,000 members of Girlguiding UK at a very special camp at Harewood House in North Yorkshire, the former home of HRH The Princess Mary, the first Royal President of the Girl Guide Association. This amazing event will offer girls hundreds of activities to choose from and will lead to another of the Centenary's spectacular celebrations, a festival of performance, creativity and music.

Foxlease, now a popular Training and Activity Centre, was the venue for the very first world camp, in 1924. Timed to coincide with the World Conference, the camp was originally intended to be for six Guides and one Guider from each country, but the organisers soon found that some countries were keen to send more. South Africa sent 37, Denmark 24, Canada 41 and Norway 18. A contingent of 37 Girl Scouts from the US were led by their founder Juliette Gordon Low

herself, and in all 40 countries were represented by 1,100 girls and women, with 600 coming from overseas.

The event required expert organisation. Special trains were laid on, Guiders offered their services as 'travellers', meeting overseas Guides and lone girls to escort them to trains, and a 'Transport Section' was set up at Foxlease to ferry girls from the station. On site there was a shop, a post office and even a ten-bed hospital for emergencies. The quantity of food shipped in was staggering – with between 61 and 116 gallons of milk, 70 joints of meat and 200 loaves of bread every day.

Girls from each nationality brought with them their own campfire songs, dances and national costumes for the amusement and fascination of all gathered there. Guides from Jerusalem sang Hebrew songs, the Swiss contingent

LEFT: Guides
at Foxlease for
the World Camp
in 1999

RIGHT: The World
Camp flag

had written and rehearsed a special song for the occasion, entitled 'À Foxlease', and the Japanese girls performed in their kimono-style uniforms. The camp ended with a grand luncheon party thrown by Princess Mary herself, and a pageant paying tribute to the great women of the past was performed. Girls dressed as Boudicca, Florence Nightingale and Queen Elizabeth I, while visiting countries represented their own heroines, such as Joan of Arc, Marie Theresa of Austria and St Elizabeth of Hungary.

The Head of the French *Eclaireuses*, who brought 22 girls to the camp, later expressed what others were feeling:

> *We have known for a long time that guiding is essentially the spirit of goodwill and sisterhood reaching across national frontiers as it reaches across barriers of class and creed. But what a difference there is between knowing a thing and actually seeing it, touching it, living it!*

One of the most remarkable world camps was the second one, held in 1939, under the shadow of a looming war in Europe. The organisers of the aptly named Pax Ting (Peace Parliament) knew that conflict was imminent but decided to go ahead in the spirit of friendship. Inspired by their faith, 4,000 girls from 32 nations, including 206 from the UK, gathered in the park of Gödöllő near Budapest. People travelled from as far afield as India and Africa, and the Hungarian hosts showed their dedication by spending extra hours in tuition, learning the languages which would be spoken by their counterparts from foreign lands. The visiting Guides had been trained and drilled for the arduous journey, and their parents, swallowing their fears about the inevitable conflict in Europe, watched with pride as they set off to represent their country.

Even the Polish contingent, who knew better than most the dark days they faced, refused to pull out, although they made one vital change at the last minute. The

WELCOME.

Dear Sister Guides and Sister Scouts!

The Hungarian Girl Scouts prepared the FIRST JAMBOREE FOR GIRL GUIDES AND GIRL SCOUTS under the name PAX-TING with the greatest pleasure and offer it from bottom of their hearts to the Girls of all the World as a Work of Love.

We have put all our strength, pride and unceasing work in the Preparation of the Great Event in order to be worthy of the Confidence given to us by the World Committee in 1937 and the Tenth World Conference in 1938.

LEFT: Pax Ting booklet

RIGHT: Girls at Pax Ting

BOTTOM: Pax Ting badge

smaller, more delicate girls were replaced with hardy Rangers, experts at outdoor pursuits and mountain climbing and they were issued with maps and special equipment. In the likely event of Poland being invaded by the Germans while they were in Hungary, they were to find their way home over the Carpathian Mountains.

After a week of fun, friendship and faultless hospitality, Pax Ting ended with the poignant sound of silver trumpets, blasted from the battlements of an ancient castle as the blue and gold trefoil flag was finally lowered. Friends from across the globe bade their farewells, knowing that forthcoming events could mean their paths would never cross again.

In September, Germany invaded Poland and war in Europe was declared. The coming together of so many at such a perilous time is the perfect illustration of the spirit of global friendship behind the world camps.

South Africa

BELOW: South
African Guides
at the World
Conference, 2008

TOP RIGHT:
33rd World
Conference logo

BOTTOM RIGHT:
Graça Machel
at the World
Conference

At the 33rd World Conference held in July 2008 in the South African city of Johannesburg delegates heard a rousing keynote speech. The speaker – Graça Machel, women's rights activist, wife of Nelson Mandela and recipient of a World Citizen Award – praised the World Association of Girl Guides and Girl Scouts (WAGGGS) for 'bringing girls together, supporting them and nurturing them through an important journey in their lives – the journey from childhood through to adolescence and into adulthood'. She then drew attention to the millions of girls who did not enjoy basic human rights and control over their own lives, and told the gathered delegates: 'I am certain that as girls and young women you have skills and confidence to change the course of destiny. You have a positive contribution to make in transforming your communities, countries and the global family. A family where difference is embraced, dignity is accorded to everyone and a family where everyone can achieve their full potential.'

Over 450 delegates representing over 100 countries travelled to the event. That it was hosted by South Africa was a fitting reminder that this diverse and troubled country was among the very first to open its doors to the Guiding Movement. It is also a country with which Robert Baden-Powell had a lifelong association.

The first troop in the country was set up soon after the 1909 Crystal Palace Rally. Miss Dorothy Rogers set up the 1st Hospital Hill troop in Johannesburg after hearing about the rally, and other companies followed, in Pretoria, Germiston, Benoni and Williamstown. In 1911 the movement spread to Middelburg, Newcastle, Pietermaritzburg, Durban, Cape Town and towns in the Orange Free State.

Throughout the dark days of apartheid, which legally segregated blacks and whites between 1948 and 1990, the Girl Guides remained a united organisation.

In 1955 the first South African Commissioner's Conference was held in Somerset West and in 1956 the South African Girl Guides Association became totally independent from London, drawing up a fresh constitution to reflect its new status.

In 1970, as part of the Diamond Jubilee Year, Olave Baden-Powell visited Cape Town, where she celebrated her 81st birthday. South African Guides presented her with the gift of a diamond, which she sold on her return to the UK in order to donate the money to world guiding.

The Girl Guides Association of South Africa has continued to flourish, with over 27,000 members to date and, true to the theme of the World Conference – join in, reach out, change lives – has been recognised for its work with women's rights and the fight against poverty, HIV and AIDS.

girls worldwide say

south africa · afrique du sud
sudáfrica 2008

33rd world conference
33e conférence mondiale
33a conferencia mundial

The United States

The spread of the Girl Guide Movement from the UK to the United States was begun by Olave and Robert Baden-Powell's close friend Juliette Gordon Low, a feisty American widow, who was almost completely deaf. In 1911, while she was living in the UK, she became an enthusiastic Guide Leader in both London and Scotland and decided to take the Movement to America. In 1912 she returned to the US and immediately called a cousin, saying 'Come right over! I've got something for the girls of Savannah, and all of America, and all the world, and we're going to start it tonight!'

Accordingly, on 12 March 1912, 18 girls were registered in the first two patrols of American Girl Guides with Juliette's niece, Margaret Gordon, named as the very first member, despite not being present at the meeting. A year later the organisation was renamed the Girl Scouts, as it is still called today.

Juliette Low died in 1927, but worked until the end of her life with Girl Guides and Girl Scouts around the world and was even buried in her beloved uniform. In 1912 she converted her carriage house into a meeting place for girls which came to be known as the Girl Scout Headquarters. She bequeathed it to the Girl Scouts of Savannah in her will.

In the 1950s the organisation was at the forefront of the fight against segregation, and began to integrate its hitherto separate groups and fight against prejudice. Civil rights leader Martin Luther King called the Girl Scouts 'a force for desegregation'. In 1969 an anti-racism initiative named Action 70 was introduced and in 1975 the Girl Scouts elected their first African-American National President, Dr Gloria D. Scott.

The GSUSA headquarters has been located in New York City since 1915 and the organisation boasts nearly 4 million members throughout the United States, Puerto Rico and the Virgin Islands as well as USA Girl Scouts Overseas in 80 countries.

ABOVE: Juliette Gordon Low

LEFT: Central Park Rally, 1920

RIGHT: US Girl Scout during the Second World War

World Thinking Day

The 22nd of February is a special day for Girl Guides and Girl Scouts everywhere. The shared birthday of Lord and Lady Baden-Powell, it is celebrated as World Thinking Day, when the girls are encouraged to remember each other and strive towards international friendship and awareness.

The date was chosen at the World Conference in 1926, with the first dedicated date taking place the following year. Now girls in the UK join millions of girls and young women from around the world to celebrate the diversity of guiding on World Thinking Day. Typical activities to celebrate the day include a focus on learning about Guides in other countries and how their lives and expectations may be different from their own.

In 1932 the World Thinking Day Fund was created to encourage girls worldwide to raise funds to support the vital work of the World Association of Girl Guides and Girls Scouts (WAGGGS) in empowering girls and young women across the globe.

Ways of celebrating Thinking Day are as diverse as the girls taking part. In 2007, 2,000 girls attended *Imagine*, an event where Rainbows, Brownies and Guides discovered the diversity of faiths in guiding in the unique setting of the British Museum. In 2008, the *World in One City* Thinking Day event attracted 6,000 members to Liverpool to learn about the cultures of the world through dance, song, music and film-making.

Elsewhere, the day is celebrated with parties and community projects. Activities can also be based on the year's theme, which in the past has included water, stopping the spread of AIDS and malaria, and discovering your potential by taking the lead.

In 1975 the World Thinking Day symbol was introduced. The trefoil at the centre represents WAGGGS, while the arrows pointing towards it signify action and direction. The symbol is circular to represent the world of guiding.

LEFT: World Thinking Day celebrations, Liverpool, 2008

RIGHT: World Thinking Day service, 1957

Embracing the world's faiths

When asked where religion came into Scouting and Guiding, Robert Baden-Powell replied:

> *It does not come in at all. It is already there. It is a fundamental factor underlying Scouting and Guiding. Though we hold no brief for any one form of belief over another, we see a way to helping all by carrying the same principle into practice as is now being employed in other branches of education.*

Guiding spread across the globe with incredible speed, which meant that girls from a rich diversity of faiths were part of the movement from the early years. African nations of all religions become members from 1910. The largely Muslim nation of Egypt joined in 1913 and Israel in 1919. The first Guide unit had opened in India in 1911; although initially it was only for British girls, guiding was on offer to Indian girls by 1916.

Robert Baden-Powell's vision was to include all races and nations, to unite them with a common framework of activities and attitudes. This far-reaching goal meant that guiding had to be adapted to suit the needs of each country and faith. An example of this was to be found in the words of the Guide Promise. The original wording of the Promise included the phrase 'to do my duty to God and my country'. In India the wording was changed from 'God' to 'Dharma', meaning the righteous path. In the UK, too, the words of the Promise evolved. In 1994 'my duty to God' was replaced with 'to love my God', thereby explicitly including members from all faiths.

Guides across the 100 years of the movement's history, as part of a global community embracing many faiths and cultures, have been empowered to explore their own beliefs and the beliefs of others in a safe, informed and non-pressurised environment just as Baden-Powell intended.

LEFT: World Thinking Day, 2005

RIGHT: World Thinking Day in Cardiff, 2004

Olave Baden-Powell

1889–1977

BELOW: Robert and Olave Baden-Powell with their grandson Robert

On 3 January 1912 Olave St Clair Soames, aged 23, embarked with her father, Harold, on a cruise aboard the ocean liner *Arcadian*, heading for New York. Though she went only reluctantly, it was a voyage that was to change not only her own life but also that of the future of the Girl Guides. Two days into the journey she met Robert Baden-Powell, who was on a world tour to promote the Scout movement, founded in 1907. Despite an age gap of over 30 years, the couple became secretly engaged aboard ship and married in October 1912. In addition to having three children, Peter, Heather and Betty, Olave Baden-Powell was to dedicate her working life to the Guide movement.

Birtley House
Bramley
Guildford
December 1st 1976   Surrey

Dear   Misa Staanbridge
        I have just redeived a beautiful bunch of flowers
from you, and   the "elderley" members of your group
of "Old Guides" with the newspaper cuttings telling me
of your bpppy 60th BIRTHDAY party held with all those
old members of your 1st Ardingly Guide Company, and
I must write at once to say THANK YOU for this kindly thougbt,
amd for the remembrance of my meeting Miss Hett, and
having had a hand in the STARTING of you all as Guides
all those years ago I

    It was so nice that you all got together for that nice
gathering the other day, and what a fine RECORD you
have , with all the Guide work done through these 60
years of servkce within our great Movement .
       1916 was the year that I began MY Guide work,
and yours must have been one of the first Companies, that
was started when I had just taken on being County Commission
    My Goodness - how things have changed since then!
And how wonderful it is to see how the Movement has grown
from that small beginning, to the immense size of to-day,
when we count our Guides in MILLIONS in 100 different
countries of the woeld !
You must be proud of yourselvs over being real PIONEERS ,
and may I offer you my congratulations on keeping touch
with alb those former members,whose names you have sent
to me with that charming note & this gift of flowers.
    It was very kind of you to write as you did, and I
thank you very much for your kindly messsage of goodwill.
    My best wishes are with you,for further prosperity
with the present day Guides in the coming years.
      Yours sincerely   *Olave Baden-Powell*

P.S.

I don't know how you managed to get those lovely flowers
tp me here , as   I had to leave my lovely home at
Hampton Court Palace three years ago. Diabetes and
Old Age have taken away the use of my LEGS, and I could not
walk   and get about ,or get anybody to cope with running
that delicious apartment that I had had 34 years of happy
busy life there .So life has changed very much for me .
   I had loved all the Guide work that I had done for
so long, and have happy memories of tours overseas as
well as haring about this country from the day of our
blissful marriage in 1912.
     It is now not possible to go about at all,
and I am well looked after in this pleasant Old Ladies
Nursing Home , and I have a few Guiders visiting me
every week , and I keep touch with what is going
on in the Movement through friends and " To-day's
Guide" and the"Council Fire" , and   any number of
other corredpondents   who write to tell me of their
busy doings .
How SPLENDID our Guiders are , and the Guides and
Brownies of to-day are just as keen and good as YOU
were in 1916 !
   I expect you had a hand in the World Conference held in
Sussex University last summer !
   I return your newspaper cutting, as you must keep it!
My desk gets rather congested with notes like yours , an
I cannot reply to them all! But YOURS,and the gift of
flowers   calls for a quick reply . Thank you for your
kind greetings,and my best wishes are with you .

      Olave Baden-Powell

From Olave's diary, 1946

West Indies, British Guiana, Cuba, Mexico, the United States, Canada and Newfoundland. Travelled 3,720 miles by sea, 6,355 miles by train, 16,610 miles by air, and 3,565 miles by road. Made 231 speeches to audiences varying in number (from 30 to 20,000), gave 62 press interviews or radio talks. Attended World Conference at Evian, France. Visited Switzerland, Czechoslovakia and Holland.

BELOW: Olave Soames chats to her future husband on board the *Arcadian*

In 1915 Olave was enrolled as a Guide in her home county of Sussex, where she set about helping to establish guiding. She was appointed Commissioner for Sussex in 1916 and wrote her first publication for the association, a booklet titled *The Girl Guide Movement*. These activities earned her the title of County Commissioner and Imperial Chief Commissioner. In 1918 she was presented with the Silver Fish, the highest Guide award. In her case, however, the fish was made of gold, as a token of the Commissioners' esteem.

Olave worked ceaselessly for the movement. For her services in the First World War she was awarded the Victory Medal. At the end of the war, realising it was time to cement global unity in guiding, she set up the Guide International and Imperial Councils, the precursor of the World Association of Girl Guides and Girl Scouts.

The 1920s saw her attend the first World Camp at Foxlease, in Hampshire, make her first radio broadcast and receive her own guide standard. In 1930, in recognition of tireless efforts in global guiding, she was acclaimed World Chief Guide at the 6th World Conference at Foxlease: she is the only person to have held this post.

On the death of Robert Baden-Powell in Kenya in 1941, a grief-stricken Olave returned to Britain. But since Pax Hill, the family home, was being used by the army, she was

granted a grace-and-favour apartment in Hampton Court Palace; she donated Pax Hill to the Guide Association to be used as a Homecraft Training Centre.

Olave travelled incessantly and was received affectionately in every country she visited. Typical of her reception is the gift presented to her by the Australian Guides: in 1958 in Australia it was suggested that when a Guide bought an ice-cream for herself she could give the equivalent money to the Guides 'to buy one for the Chief Guide'. In the first year of the campaign £300 was contributed. Olave chose to spend it not on herself: the money was used instead to send books on guiding written in Spanish from Mexico to Guides in Argentina, Uruguay, Chile, Ecuador, Colombia, Panama, Costa Rica, Nicaragua, El Salvador and Guatemala. 'Blew the £300,' she said later. 'It was the greatest fun.'

She died on 25 June 1977. After a funeral service at Bentley Church in Hampshire, her ashes were taken to Kenya to be placed next to her husband's.

FAR LEFT: Olave Baden-Powell standard

LEFT: Portrait by Claude Harris

RIGHT: Olave in Germany celebrating the Jubilee, 1960

A Warm Welcome

RIGHT: Guides with disabilities from Queen Mary's Hospital, Carshalton, at a 1924 camp

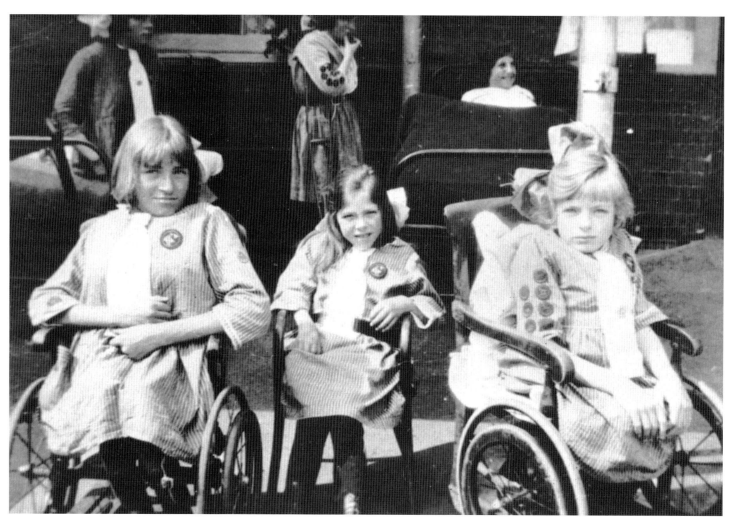

Lord Baden-Powell's dream was to bring youngsters together, regardless of class, race and social background. His all-inclusive vision was perfectly voiced in his attitude towards uniform, one of the characteristics that sets the Guides and Scouts apart from many youth groups. 'A like uniform hides all differences and makes for equality,' he said. 'More important still, it covers the differences of country and race and makes all feel that they are members of one organisation.'

The majority of the earliest Guides trained in first aid, stretcher work and signalling, and enjoyed activities such as camping, cycling, gymnastics and even sailing; but the need to include and adapt for children with special needs was evident from day one.

In fact, the first group – then called Girl Scouts – formed as early as 1909 in a hospital in Carshalton, Surrey. Queen Mary's was the largest children's hospital in Europe and one Dr Griffen felt that the children could benefit from a troop of Boy and Girl Scouts. The move proved so popular that guiding activities at the hospital eventually grew to include five Guide companies, six Brownie packs and a Ranger company. In 1910, a unit for children with hearing and speech problems was established in the Royal Cross School in Preston. Within five years a troop for blind children was set up at a school in Liverpool as was a unit for children with other disabilities in Newcastle.

LEFT: Senior Section members using sign language, 2008

RIGHT: Lady Helen Newcome, whose work led to the establishment of the Extension Branch

At this point, each new company was adapting the official programme to suit the needs and abilities of the members, but in 1919 all that changed. Lady Helen Newcome, a newly appointed Head of Kindred Societies, discovered among her predecessor's papers the outline of a plan to extend guiding to children with disabilities, children with learning difficulties and to those in orphanages and rescue homes. She called a meeting that resulted in the formation of the Extension Branch, a central committee to oversee the companies, with Lady Newcome as head and Mrs Fryer (later Lady Fryer) as secretary.

A year later an audit concluded that 22 companies were already running in special schools and hospitals for the blind, deaf and those with mobility problems, three in institutions for those with learning difficulties, 12 in rescue homes and 16 in orphanages and workhouses.

The branch then published the booklet *Guiding in Institutions*, which was distributed to public voluntary societies and institutions. Badges were adapted and a set of alternative tests put in place to allow less able-bodied Guides to complete their Second Class, First Class and Interest badges. New proficiency badges included handicraft and Braille, and in the 1922 annual report the introduction of the Nurse Cavell award, for outstanding courage in the midst of suffering, was announced. In 1921, reportedly in response to the comments of a little girl paralysed from the waist down who said she longed to be a Guide, the Post Guides was set up. The scheme, linked to the Invalid Children's Aid Association, allowed those who were confined to their own homes to join the movement, and Mrs Fryer became the captain of the 1st Post Company.

BELOW: Scottish Post Guide Camp at the Trefoil School in 1962

The communication with the girls seemed to have such a beneficial effect that one doctor wrote to ask what it was the Post Guides were doing, because whatever it was his patient was not only happier but had experienced an improvement in her general health. After consulting with other doctors, who agreed on the benefits, steps were taken to ensure that all those dealing with housebound children, from physicians to clergymen, were aware of the existence of the Post Guides. A quarterly periodical called *The Bluebird* was started to give Post Guiders new ideas for letters to their unit, and to provide general interest articles.

Post Guiding had some remarkable success stories. One girl of 15, who had never been to school because of ill-health and had lost the use of her legs, was taught to read and write by her Leader and was taken to the weekly meeting to

LEFT: A Guide kayaking

RIGHT: A Rainbow taking part in a sports day event

interact with other children for the first time. She was also taught a craft, and in selling her work was able to contribute for the first time to her family's meagre income.

In 1925, after a hospital almoner asked if anything could be done for younger children who were confined, the Post Brownies was established.

By 1931, there were over 140 Post Guide and Ranger companies in the UK and the idea had also spread to several other countries. Extension companies had expanded too, with 450 in the UK and further units in South Africa, Australia, New Zealand, India, Canada, Holland, British Guiana, France, Finland, Norway, the US and Switzerland. Meanwhile, because of the huge success of the Extension Branch, it was decided in 1924 that the companies in rescue homes, orphanages and poor law schools should fall into a different group; this was put into place with the establishment of the Auxiliary Branch.

Innovations in the early years of the Extension Branch included a Braille library and a mauve circle added to the badges of girls who took alternative and adapted tests. Blind Guider Miss Jean Robinson became the editor of the first Braille magazine for Guides and Scouts and, in 1927, the first camp for Post Rangers took place.

RIGHT: Scottish
Post Guide Camp
at the Trefoil
School in 1962

FAR LEFT:
Disability
Awareness badge
for Brownies

FAR RIGHT: A girl
and a volunteer at
a camp for children
with disabilities

In the following decade an experimental school for children with disabilities was set up, and was staffed entirely by Guiders. The Trefoil School, which opened in 1939, took boys and girls from all over Scotland and was open all year round for those who could not be cared for at home.

Activities for Guides with disabilities continued to grow, and included a camp at Beaconsfield in Buckinghamshire in 1957, for the Centenary of Lord Baden-Powell's birth, and an educational cruise for 14 members in 1963, donated by Christmas card printers T. E. Webb.

The 1970s saw a huge boom in activities for Guides with disabilities, with a special Olympics in Munich in 1972 and a group of blind members climbing Ben Nevis three years later. All the girls took part in the 1979 International Year of the Child, in association with UNESCO.

The 1981 International Year of the Disabled saw an initiative called *Enabled Though Disabled,* in which girls were encouraged to look at their own neighbourhood through the eyes of someone with a disability. They took into account access and communication problems experienced by others in their community and came up with ideas on how to make life easier. The project was a great demonstration of the movement's long-held belief in inclusion for all and celebration of diversity.

Today Girlguiding UK's commitment to helping girls with special needs to get the most out of their membership remains firmly in place. The programme of activities is sufficiently flexible for most girls and adults of any ability to participate; special funding is available to assist them; and some activity centres have been adapted to their needs. In 2004 the Disability Awareness Challenge badge was introduced. This badge encourages Brownies and Guides to imagine life as a person with disabilities, through writing stories and plays, playing games with restricted limbs and designing toys for a child with special needs.

Larking about

Woodlarks campsite sprawls across 12 acres in the Surrey countryside and provides accessible camping for people with all kinds of disabilities. Most Guides who visit the yearly summer camps sleep under canvas, and two of the tents include a wooden floor for the use of hoists and power points for those who need breathing apparatus. For Guides who are unable to sleep outside there is indoor accommodation and activities that they can enjoy include swimming, bivouacking, trampolining and archery.

The site was opened in 1930 as a gift from the Strover family, who lived nearby. The initial donation from Colonel Strover, his wife Dorothea and friend Christina Tisdall bought three acres of land, but the charitable trust they set up received enough funds over the ensuing years to buy a further nine acres.

A Helping Hand

For over 60 years, until 1986, the Handcraft Depot helped girls with disabilities earn a living by selling their own work. Opened in 1925 by Mrs and Miss Hodson in a room in Regent Street, the depot transferred to Guide Headquarters two years later.

Workers were provided with wool, for knitted items, but provided their own materials for making toys, and the goods were sent in whenever they were completed. They were then sold at Association shops, at agricultural shows and at County, Division and District meetings, with the girls being paid at the end of each month.

The Extension Branch Fund was used in 1933 to set up a scholarship scheme so that talented girls could receive formal training in their craft; 17 scholarships were awarded in the first year. However, the scheme was dropped during the Second World War and was deemed too impractical to revive afterwards.

The depot proved a roaring success, however, allowing girls who were unable to get jobs to seize a precious nugget of independence. One girl apparently proved so talented at toy design that it was reported, in 1938, that she had landed a job as a designer in a London toy factory through her work for the depot. In 1935 the British Red Cross put in an order for wool mascots to sell on Red Cross Day – some 50,000 of them.

The war years saw the depot's workers pouring their talents into a 'Make Do and Mend' service rather than making luxury goods, and they were a great help to the forces as well as evacuee children.

By 1977, because of the increasing efforts of local authorities to get people with disabilities into ordinary jobs, the number of depot workers had fallen to 12. By 1986 legislation had been passed requiring employers to take on staff with disabilities, and so the decision was made to close the depot.

RIGHT: A leather
dog toy made
by a Ranger for
the depot

Guiding for all

A number of special initiatives have been developed over the years to include girls and young women in guiding from around the UK.

'For no girl can the Guide Movement be of greater value than for the delinquent schoolgirl.' Such was the conclusion of the 1920 report *Guiding in Institutions*, which continued: 'During the last few years quite a number of institutions have started Patrols and all who have seen anything of genuine Guide work in such places will wish that it should form a feature of the training in every home for orphan, neglected, or delinquent girls.'

By then it was clear that the appeal of the Girl Guides transcended all class and social barriers, as Lord Baden-Powell had intended. At the beginning of the decade there were 12 companies and two Brownie packs in industrial schools, eight companies in penitentiaries and 52 companies in charitable institutions. In 1923, a pack had formed in a borstal and two more in reformatory schools. With this special section growing rapidly it was agreed that the Auxiliary Branch should be formed to take over the work with troubled and underprivileged children, and in 1927 a Guide camp was held for these girls.

Mrs Crichton Miller, then head of the branch, wrote in her 1928 report:

Nowhere is Guiding more urgently needed than among the girls found in penitentiaries, rescue homes and such institutions: but also nowhere has it to contend with such difficulties. [Some] 25 companies exist, run by a devoted band of Guiders who have to face the difficulty of dealing with such girls. In addition there is the complication

" Prison Commission,
" Home Office,
" Whitehall, S.W.1.
" 17th November, 1919.

" MADAM,

" I am directed by the Prison Commissioners to inform you that sufficient time has now elapsed since the Girl Guide Movement was introduced into the Aylesbury Borstal Institution for Girls in April last, to enable them to come to the conclusion that it has been a great success, the inmates taking much interest in it and the authorities of the Institution being of opinion that highly favourable results are likely to accrue.

" The Commissioners have therefore directed me to express their thanks for the assistance you so kindly gave in the matter and their appreciation of the interest you took in it.

" I am, Madam,
" Your obedient Servant,
" A. J. WALL,
" *Secretary*.

" Lady Baden-Powell,
" Pax Hill,
" Bentley, Hants."

RIGHT: A member
of a Switch group
in Folkestone
having a go
at horseriding

of institution life and regulations and the limited time available for Guiding and, above all, the problem of finding for her the right type of company when she goes out into the world once more.

By the 1950s social change led to a drop in the number of companies, to just nine. Many girls who still lived in approved schools were encouraged to join units outside, and in 1959 the Auxiliary Branch was disbanded. The movement continued to reach out to underprivileged children through an extensive Inner Cities programme. In 1958, for example, a Travelling Commissioner was appointed to help set up units in new towns and housing estates.

Factory workers were another social group that benefited from forming their own companies in the early part of the century. At the Luton engineering firm George Kent Ltd, for example, the 1st Luton Girl Guides was formed for the workers in the factory. During the First World War, the firm was engaged in the manufacture of shell fuses for guns and a badge was introduced with the letters GK to signify the girls' work.

Between the wars, retired Field Marshal Lord Douglas Haig worked tirelessly with the British Legion to help ex-servicemen and to promote the Poppy Appeal. His wife, Lady Haig, ran the poppy factory in Richmond, and between 1929 and 1936 relied on the attached Guide unit, the 3rd Richmond Hill (Lady Haig's Own), to collect moss and poppy seeds.

More recently, in 1992 the Reach Out project saw officers appointed in London, Newcastle and Liverpool to promote guiding in inner cities. Further officers joined the scheme, a year later in Nottingham, Canning Town, Essex, Norton St Philip, Bristol and Staffordshire; and in 1994 the scheme expanded into the Stirling and Falkirk areas.

In 2006 the Big Lottery-funded Switch Project began, introducing guiding to communities that traditionally had little or no experience of guiding opportunities. Switch groups enabled girls and young women to plan their own programmes and to try new activities. Many groups became part of local guiding at the end of the Switch Project.

BELOW:
A Switch trip to Waddow, 2008

By Royal Appointment

FAR RIGHT: Guide badge bearing the picture of the Princess's playhouse

RIGHT: Princess Elizabeth, aged eight, stands in front of the Little House, a gift from the Guides of Wales

In 1937, shortly after the coronation of HM King George VI, a lady called Violet Synge had a memorable phone conversation with Marion Crawford, the legendary nanny to the 11-year-old HRH The Princess Elizabeth and 7-year-old HRH Princess Margaret Rose. 'Crawfie', as she was affectionately known, requested that Mrs Synge set up a new Guide company to include the new heir to the throne and her younger sister. The request had come directly from the Queen, who had recently become Patron of the Association. 'You will find them just like any ordinary little girl,' Crawfie told Mrs Synge, who later confessed in her book *Royal Guides*, 'I had not believed her at the time.'

Having agreed to the task, Mrs Synge was duly invited for tea with Princess Elizabeth who 'By her complete charm and naturalness … helped me overcome my gaucherie, trotting round the table with bread and butter or with buns whenever she saw my plate empty.'

As they got to know one another, the door opened and in wandered the 'minute figure' of Margaret, who had come to see what was going on:

After I had greeted her with a solemn salute and handshake (bending double in the process) and resumed my seat, Princess Elizabeth called 'Come here Margaret!' Princess Margaret toddled over and was told, 'Show Captain your legs!' The cotton frock was crumpled up and the legs duly displayed. 'There,' said Princess Elizabeth, proudly, 'don't you call those a fine pair of hiking legs?' Whatever I said I couldn't help thinking 'They are undoubtedly sturdy, but they are very short!'

The meeting was the beginning of a lifelong devotion to the Brownies and Guides from both Princesses: Princess Margaret became President in 1965 and remained so until her death in 2002, and the Queen became Patron in 1952, a position she holds to this day.

The 1st Buckingham Palace Brownie Pack and Guide Company began in June 1937, with 14 Guides and Brownies recruited from cousins, friends and children of the staff at the Palace. The Princesses apart, the members were, at first, determined to be on their best behaviour so it was an orderly affair, as Mrs Synge recalled: 'From the

The Little House

The Little House (Y Bwthyn Bach) was a beautiful thatched playhouse given to Princess Elizabeth on her sixth birthday by the people of Wales, and subsequently erected at the Royal Lodge in Windsor. In 1940, the Princess gave permission for the Little House to be used as the design for the Little House Emblem, which was to be awarded to a Guide for gaining the badges of Cook, Child Nurse, Needlewoman, Laundress, Homemaker and Hostess.

outset I was met with a problem never met in my previous 15 years' experience of guiding, namely, to incite the children to let themselves go, to run, to climb, and to do the things that an 11–14-year-old is usually all too willing to do.'

However, the barriers soon broke down, with games, chases and activities carried out in the vast gardens of Buckingham Palace, and in December the Princesses were officially enrolled by their aunt, HRH The Princess Mary, who was then the President of the Guide Association. The pack would

continue to meet until 1939, when war necessitated the Royal Family's move to Balmoral, where the two Princesses joined local companies.

In 1942, the 1st Buckingham Palace company reconvened at Windsor, where they would meet until the end of the war, and Princess Elizabeth became Patrol Leader of the Swallows. Princess Margaret was now able to move up to join her sister in the Guides, and on 23 February 1943, she became Patrol Leader of the Bullfinches. Despite the war, the Princesses joined camps each year, although they were not always able

to sleep under canvas because of the dangers of the ever-increasing German bombs.

The 1944 camp, at Frogmore, brought two special visitors – the King and Queen. The campers, prepared as always, had been provided with special crockery. 'Judge of my horror,' recalled Mrs Synge, 'when Princess Margaret (Leader of the Mess Patrol) presented the Queen with a chipped enamel mug from the handle of which dangled a long piece of greasy string, and the King with an awful-looking object the size of a young bath!' The Quartermaster later explained

that Princess Margaret could not be persuaded to hand her parents the best china because the others were 'more campy'. The King and Queen, however, were delighted with the healthy activities of their daughter and remarked on the order and tidiness of the camp.

Before the Princesses moved up to Sea Rangers in 1943 and 1946, respectively, they both gained First Class badges. Among the interest badges earned by Princess Elizabeth were Interpreter, Swimmer, Dancer, Horsewoman, Cook, Child Nurse and Needlewoman,

ABOVE: Princess Elizabeth as a Sea Ranger on camp at Frogmore, 1944

LEFT: Princess Elizabeth and Princess Margaret as Sea Rangers

RIGHT: Princess Margaret draws her ration on camp, 1944

ABOVE: Silver brooch presented to the Queen on her 21st birthday

while her sister gained Artist, Athlete, Child Nurse, Cook, Emergency Helper, Homemaker, Horsewoman, Hostess, Interpreter, Laundress, Needlewoman and Pioneer.

In 1946, the girls spent four days aboard the training ship MTB (Motor Torpedo Boat) 630 at Dartmouth, performing the same duties as their crew, including peeling potatoes and scrubbing down the decks. The same year Princess Elizabeth became the Chief Ranger of the British Empire.

At 20, the future Queen was still taking part in camps whenever possible and, on one occasion, she brought her fiancé, Lieutenant Mountbatten (later the Duke of Edinburgh), to meet her delighted crew. On her 21st birthday, Princess Elizabeth was presented with a floral spray brooch set with diamonds. Each spray was in the shape of a trefoil, mounted in gold and platinum, and tied with a diamond bow. The upper trefoil, set with topaz and diamonds, represented Brownies; the left-hand trefoil, set with rubies and diamonds, represented Rangers; and

the right-hand trefoil, set with sapphires and diamonds, represented Guides.

Even as Princess Elizabeth walked up the aisle, on 20 November 1947, the Guides were represented in the form of two bridesmaids and former Buckingham Palace Company members Lady Mary Cambridge and Lady Elizabeth Lambert. Six crew members from the SRS *Duke of York* (the Sea Ranger ship that both Princesses Elizabeth and Margaret had been part of the crew of) were at Westminster Abbey and another 23 members of the crew were on the forecourt of Buckingham Palace, while 100 Rangers wished her well from outside the Palace. The 500 lb wedding cake was made from ingredients sent by 25,000 Australian Guides, and the trefoils of the Guides and Sea Rangers decorated the top tier – which was kept and in 1948 used as part of Prince Charles's christening cake. Wedding presents from the members, who voluntarily contributed a penny or threepence each, included a Chippendale desk and a Carlton House writing table (c. 1780) as well as

Princess Margaret's Banner

In 1965, the year Princess Margaret became President, permission was granted for a personal standard or banner to be made for her. She chose the rectangular banner shape and Mrs B. Martineau, County Commissioner for Birmingham, undertook the design and needlework with Mrs Brown of Warwick, President of the Local Association, Mrs M. Wilkinson and Miss B. Chatwin, assistant County Commissioner for Birmingham. All were past or present students at the Bourneville School of Art. The finished product, which is mostly appliqué work with some detailed stitching, took 1,250 hours to make and is now displayed at Foxlease.

1st quarter – Gold Trefoil on Guide Blue

2nd quarter – Gold Lion of England on Red field and crowned with Princess's Coronet

3rd quarter – Four symbols on a Gold field: Tudor Rose for England, Scottish Thistle, Red Hand of Ulster, Red Dragon of Wales

4th quarter – Repeat of 1st

kitchen equipment. A chiming clock by Robert Banks (c. 1760) was sent to HRH Prince Philip. Six years later, at the Queen's coronation, the movement was once more represented, and two Guides from the Commonwealth were invited to the ceremony. A badge was also issued to commemorate the event, and Princess Margaret replaced her sister as the Chief Ranger of the British Empire.

In 1960 Queen Elizabeth the Queen Mother became Patron of the Trefoil Guild, and a year later her granddaughter, HRH Princess Anne, enrolled as a Guide, having spent two years as a Brownie.

In 1965, following the death of Princess Mary at the age of 68, Princess Margaret became the President of

the Association. In almost 40 years as the head of the movement she proved, with her deep involvement in all aspects of its activities, that she was much more than a figurehead. She undertook numerous engagements each year, all over the UK, and whenever possible attended council meetings to take the chair. She frequently visited Guide centres such as Glenbrook in Derbyshire, Lorne in Ulster and Foxlease in Hampshire, and in 1975 opened the World Conference in Brighton. Ten years later she was present at many of the celebrations marking the Guides' 75th anniversary and opened Guide week by handing

a flame of friendship to representatives from all nine UK regions at a ceremony at Buckingham Palace.

Princess Margaret's love of the Guides lasted throughout her life; and at the Memorial Service held for her in April 2002, as many as 90 members of the Association were present to show that the feeling was mutual. In her memory, the Princess Margaret Memorial Fund was launched and the money collected was used to provide resources at the Training and Activity Centres.

BELOW:
HRH The Countess of Wessex meets a Guide at the Changing the World launch in 2008

The current President of Girlguiding UK, HRH The Countess of Wessex, took on the mantle on 17 May 2003, a year after the death of Princess Margaret. A former Brownie herself, she made her first official visit to Commonwealth Headquarters (CHQ) in September of that year to present 35 Queen's Guide brooches, and is now a regular face at Guide events throughout the country.

Her appointment reflects the long association between the Guides and the royal family that began almost 100 years ago. Princess Louise, the Duchess of Argyll and daughter of Queen Victoria, became a patron in 1911, and nine years later her niece, Princess Mary, succeeded Agnes Baden-Powell as President. Princess Mary, the daughter of George V, was already the President of the Norfolk Guides, and both Agnes and Robert Baden-Powell felt she would a valuable asset as figurehead for the whole organisation. She remained President and a devotee of the Girl Guide Association until her death, and was tireless in her efforts to promote the movement for which she held a deep affection.

A wedding gift

When Princess Mary announced her engagement to the Earl of Harewood in 1921, the 215,000 Guides and Brownies raised £4,000 in pennies and presented her with a wedding gift of a trefoil in rubies and diamonds and silver models of Girl Guides. She was also to receive the gift of £8,000 from the Marys of the Empire, donated by all those who shared her name throughout the British territories. The generous Princess was determined to donate the whole amount to the Girl Guides but, after a deputation from the Marys begged her to choose a personal gift, she agreed to put just over £2,000 towards a pearl necklace and then donate the balance. However, she also handed over £4,000 of the proceeds from an exhibition of her wedding presents.

In January 1922, a month before the wedding, an American lady called Mrs Archbold Sanderson wrote to the executive of the Guides offering them a large house in Hampshire with its 60 acres as a gift. The Guides had been camping at the uninhabited property, on the edge of the New Forest, for 11 years, but there was hesitation over the generous offer, because of concerns about upkeep. But the money pledged by Princess Mary, and the flurry of donations that this in turn inspired, meant that the establishment and upkeep of a training centre at the house was possible. Foxlease was furnished by Guides from all over the world: Scotland took on the drawing room, India the dining room and Chinese Guides donated a gong. A Guide Leader, Mrs Storrow, donated many furnishings while American Guide founder, Mrs Juliette Low, moved in for several weeks to oversee the renovations.

Today Foxlease plays host to hundreds of Guides in full-board accommodation in Princess Mary House, camping and self-catering accommodation, and boasts conference facilities and a heated swimming pool. Visitors can enjoy archery, climbing, abseiling, canoeing, kayaking, low ropes, high ropes, crate challenge and team-building activities. In 2005 a new adventure house called Princess Margaret House was built and officially opened by the President.

'You get lots of things to do at Foxlease!'
says 11-year-old Georgina.

BELOW: Foxlease

Agnes Baden-Powell

LEFT: Agnes in uniform

RIGHT: Agnes with her mother, Henrietta Baden-Powell

Agnes Baden-Powell was instrumental in the foundation and early development of the Girl Guide movement. Always close to her brother, after the Crystal Palace Rally in 1909 she set up the first organisation for the girls. The next year she formed the Girl Guides Association and took over the role of President, and in 1912 published the female version of *Scouting for Boys*, entitled *How Girls Can Help to Build Up the Empire*.

In this time of sexual inequality and the rise of the suffragette movement, led by Emmeline and Christabel Pankhurst, many in society were suspicious of the Guide movement, believing it would turn their little girls into tomboys and feminists. Though in private Agnes may have shared some of the Pankhursts' views on female emancipation, she was careful in the message she put across in public; and in fact one of her many attributes was her ability to combat prejudice against girls wearing uniform and taking part in outdoor activities. In the early guiding magazines she projected the movement as a womanly organisation in which education would make the girls better housewives, more capable in all womanly arts from cooking, washing and sick nursing to the management of children. Yet she also encouraged them to learn all they could about motor cars, learn to drive, and to aspire to a career rather than just a job. In 1920 Agnes resigned as President and took on the position of Vice-President, continuing to be an active part of the organisation, even attending the International Camp in Ulster and sleeping under canvas at the age of 77. She died on 2 June 1945, aged 86.

LEFT: Agnes with Guides at a camp

Artistic Licence

RIGHT: The famous Beatrix Potter painting

FAR LEFT: C. R. Mansell wrote many Guide stories, including *The Littlest Guide*, in the 1940s

FAR RIGHT: *The Third Rucksack Book* was published in 1957

"Peter Rabbit and the Guides at Troutbeck Park."
from Beatrix Potter
May 31st 1928

In honour of a birthday girl in the company, Beatrix painted a beautiful watercolour of Peter Rabbit being handed a cake by a Guide. The picture, which appears in the log book kept by the company, has the caption 'Peter Rabbit and the Guides at Troutbeck Park'. Alongside the illustration an entry from one of the girls present reads: 'Mrs Heelis came to tea with us. It was Margaret Buchanan's birthday. She had to work hard cutting up a big birthday cake.'

As early as 1912, the year Agnes Baden-Powell published the first handbook – *How Girls Can Help to Build Up the Empire* – a girls' novel called *Terry the Girl Guide* appeared. The story by Dorothea Moore gave an interesting insight into the adventures of the first Patrols.

It was Penelope who at once lifted the Patrol into its proper place, an altitude above the jeers of the less patriotic, by the stirring couplet, pinned to the boxroom door when weather required meetings to be held indoors.

*'The Manor Guides are made of girls
That scorneth to be flabby.
They think Imperully; they think
Victory of Westminster Abbey.'*

Writers and artists alike have long had a fascination with guiding, and their portrayal of Guides and Brownies shows how widespread the appeal of the movement is.

In 1928 the girls of the Chorlton-cum-Hardy Company were thrilled when one Mrs Heelis came to tea. The lady in question, otherwise known as Beatrix Potter, often allowed the girls to camp on her extensive farmland in Troutbeck and Hawkshead, in the picturesque surroundings of the Lake District.

In her Foreword, Agnes commented: 'I expect this delightful Terry the Girl Guide will have great vogue. Each succeeding event is so thrilling that one cannot put the book down.' Moore, who was a Guide Commissioner, repeated the success with many more titles including *Judy Patrol Leader*, *Guide Gilly* and *Greta of the Guides*.

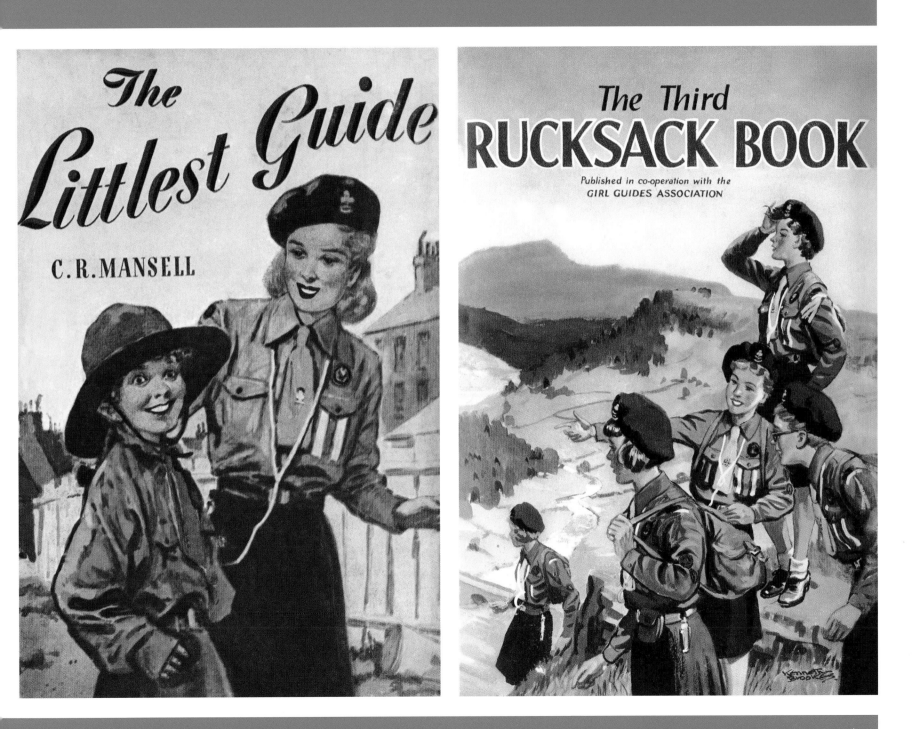

RUPERT SEES THE GUIDES' CAMP

Quite suddenly the cap appears.
"Hooray, that's lucky!" Edward cheers.

The cap is rescued, safe and sound.
Then Rupert says, "It's spinning round!"

That cap is far too wet to wear.
"Let's show the Guides," says Rupert Bear.

Smiles Pauline, "Yes, you'd better try
And see if you can get it dry."

Rupert has hardly spoken when they see the cap again. It shoots out of the water a few yards ahead of them. "Hoorah! Now we can get it!" cries Rupert. Quickly he finds a stick, kneels down on the bank, and reaches out to catch the cap. "Here it is!" he shouts, holding it up for Edward to see. "It's dripping wet but—" Rupert stops short as he notices that the cap is spinning like a top. "What ever has made it do that?" he exclaims. "Maybe something happened while it was in the whirlpool," murmurs Edward. "Perhaps it will stop soon. But how can I dry it?" Rupert is lost for an answer, but a little later they see the Girl Guides, who have camped in a meadow. "Look, they have a fire!" cries Rupert. "That's just what we need." The Guides are very surprised to see the strange cap, which still spins merrily on the end of the stick. "You certainly can't wear it while it's so wet," says Pauline. Edward is told to sit in front of the fire and dry the cap.

In 1923 Robert Baden-Powell's friend Rudyard Kipling published *Land and Sea Stories for Scouts and Guides*, a collection of short stories in which, despite the title's inclusion of the female section of the Movement, all the protagonists were boys. But the 1920s also saw a glut of Girl Guide stories from such authors as Nancy M. Hayes, who wrote *The Caravan Patrol* and *The Plucky Patrol*, and Winifred Darch, with such titles as *Cicely Bassett Patrol Leader*.

Mrs Osborn Hann embarked on a series of Guide stories, including the Peg stories, which followed the heroine through Brownies, in *Peg Juniors* and as a Guide in *Peg's Patrol* and *Peg the Ranger*. Frances Nash wrote the Audrey series, beginning with *How Audrey Became a Girl Guide*, as well as writing Brownie adventures such as *Brownies and Boggarts* (1924). In 1942 these two stalwarts of guiding stories combined their talents to produce a wartime novel entitled *Merrily Makes Things Move*, which followed the adventures of evacuee Guides from London.

Since then the plucky girls of the Brownies and Guides have cropped up in many a tale, and sometimes in the most unlikely places – such as the Rupert Bear cartoon serialised in the *Daily Express*. In Number 49 of the *Rupert Adventure Series*, dated 1963, Rupert and his friend Edward visit the Guides, who are camping at Nutwood.

RIGHT: Magazines published for Guides and Brownies

LEFT: No. 49 in the *Daily Express* Rupert the Bear Series, 1963

FAR RIGHT: *Peg's Patrol* was first published around 1924

Like novels and handbooks, magazines and annuals have played a huge part in guiding through the ages. *Guiding*, formally *The Guider* and *Girl Guides' Gazette*, has been published without interruption since January 1914 for the adult membership, while from 1921 girls could enjoy *Today's Guide*, which later became *The Guide* and was finally renamed *Guide Patrol* before ceasing publication in 1994. *The Brownie* magazine, published from 1962 to 2005, was especially for the 7–10-year-old membership, and a Rangers periodical ran from 1947 until 1974. Guides also had their own annuals between 1951 and 1993 and the Brownies since 1958. Robert Baden-Powell was a prolific artist and sculptor in his own right and often lent his talents to the Association's magazines, as well as to Scouting publications. (And, incidentally, his horse Black Prince provided the inspiration for Lucy Kemp-Welch's famous illustrations of *Black Beauty*, the children's novel by Anna Sewell.)

After writing the *1918 Girl Guiding: The Official Handbook* Baden-Powell also illustrated the cover with a charming picture of a Guider dancing with two young girls. The joyous tableau was not, however, universally popular, with one letter to the *Girl Guides' Gazette* claiming that the book's 'dignity is entirely marred by the rowdy disfigurement on the outside'. Nevertheless, the image was chosen to grace the 21st birthday stamps released in 1932. The celebration was postponed from the real anniversary in 1931 because of an economic crisis.

Celebrated artist Margaret Tarrant, best known for her fairy tale illustrations and fairy postcards, designed many beautiful greetings cards for the Guide movement, starting in 1920. Brownies were usually depicted in the company of fairies and pixies, while Guides were shown partaking in activities such as camping, collecting wood or doing a good turn.

Fellow artist and friend Molly Brett also designed cards, as did the illustrator Grace Shelton. In her set of six postcards the prolific artist Millicent Sowerby showed in each card a girl performing a good deed, with an accompanying poem. For example, the gardening verse read:

ABOVE: Stamps
from 1932

RIGHT: A postcard
by Millicent
Sowerby

In Spring a gardening we go
And work with spade and rake and hoe,
And when we've pulled up all the weeds
We choose and plant out favourite seeds.

WEARING APRONS NEAT AND WHITE~
MAKING PASTRY FIRM AND LIGHT ⚬ · ⚬
SOUP AND CAKES AND PUDDINGS, ~ LOOK
WE CAN SHOW YOU HOW TO COOK. ⚬ · ⚬

WHAT'S WRONG
WITH THIS
PICTURE
?

FAR LEFT:
'Queen of the Brownies', by Margaret Tarrant

LEFT:
Fougasse poster

Stamp of success

In March 1982 the Girl Guides featured on stamps issued to honour youth organisations. The set of four represented the Girls' Brigade, Boys' Brigade, Scout Movement and the Guides, with the Guides appearing on the 29p stamp. To mark the Centenary of Girlguiding UK, Royal Mail is producing a special set of attractive stamps in 2010.

More recently, famous artists and cartoonists have lent their humour to the Guide movement, most notably the Second World War propaganda supremo Fougasse (whose real name was Cyril Kenneth Bird). His recruitment poster, aimed at attracting new Guide Leaders, showed a girl waving her fellow Guides off to camp with the caption 'What's wrong with this picture?' The idea was that she was unable to go because of the shortage of Leaders.

Going for GOLD 1

GOLD

Guiding Overseas Linked with Development, or GOLD for short, was introduced in 1991, and since then its far-reaching projects have ensured that Guides from different countries work together to improve the lives of others. Each year small groups of girls aged 18 to 30 travel together to meet Guides from other countries and work on projects within their communities. The programme has included trips to Belarus, Cambodia, Egypt, Fiji, Honduras, Hungary, Kenya, Madagascar, Pakistan, Russia, Serbia, Slovakia, South Africa, Sri Lanka, Uganda and Ukraine. To be chosen for the GOLD programme girls attend a team-building and activity weekend and then apply to take part. Each 'GOLDie' has to raise her own funds for participating in the project.

RIGHT: A GOLD project participant teaches girls a craft in Fiji in 2006

LEFT: Emma Joyce on her GOLD project in Honduras in 2008

RIGHT: Activities with the Guides and Brownies of Fiji in 2006

Emma Joyce spent three weeks in Honduras in August 2008:

It was the fourth year of a five-year project which was originally just about HIV and AIDS but we developed it to include teenage pregnancy and sexual health awareness.

We had two briefings on the practical aspects, what we were going to do and how we were going to do it. There were six of us and we were able to plan a programme drawing on publications that Girlguiding UK and other outside organisations have produced.

It was amazing. Every project is unique in terms of how you get along, how you cope with quite a demanding project, because it can really test you in particular ways. For instance, we had to use translators but we didn't always have them available.

We went through every kind of accommodation, from tents to plush hotel rooms, and we all had very long days. Although it's a challenge, it's incredibly rewarding. It was exhausting but wonderful.

When you're running a camp for sixty girls in Honduras, and you're able to come away knowing they've learned something, it's a great feeling.

2

A Guiding Voice

Girls Shout Out

As well as practical skills and a girl-only space in which to thrive, Girlguiding UK is committed to giving girls and young women a voice in society – starting from the Crystal Palace Rally, where they spoke out. In recent years *Girls Shout Out!* surveys have been carried out to gauge the feelings of young people on the important issues of the day. Chief Guide Liz Burnley observes: 'At a time when young people are too often stereotyped, criticised and denied a voice, we hope that our report *Girls Shout Out!* will be an opportunity for young women's voices to be heard.'

Girl Power

Watch out world – Girl Power is here! One in ten young Guides wants to be Prime Minister, according to the first *Girls Shout Out!* report, published in March 2007, and 90 per cent of 10–15-year-olds believe they can do any job they want.

The survey took in the views of 3,200 guiding members aged 5 to 25 and found that Olympic Gold Medallist Kelly Holmes was the top role model. And while 95 per cent named Kate Moss and Victoria Beckham as the greatest influences on young women, only 2 per cent thought they were positive role models!

What Girlguiding UK's members think

81% say they won't depend on their partners financially

30% aspire to be doctors

12% aspire to be politicians

39% worry they won't get paid as much as men

Source: *Girls Shout Out!*, March 2007

Although the girls believed they had the opportunity to do any job, two-thirds felt that women had not achieved equality with men and a third thought they were given different careers advice because of their gender. Four out of five older members said they would not be financially dependent on a partner, while 90 per cent said they would return to work after having children.

Equality in society was also an issue, with 73 per cent saying girls were stigmatised for behaviour considered acceptable for boys, such as binge-drinking.

The girls also revealed the extent of cyber-bullying, with 38 per cent of those over 10 saying they knew of malicious rumours spread online about someone they know and half the over-16s saying they knew someone who had received an abusive email.

Body worries in under-10s

Self-esteem:
Girls shout out!

Under ten and under pressure?

A research report by
Girlguiding UK

Girlguiding UK

A survey among Brownies revealed shocking results on body image in the under-10s. The second *Girls Shout Out!* survey, titled *Under Ten and Under Pressure*, revealed that 7–10 year-olds equate being slim and pretty with being clever, happy and popular. In the focus groups, conducted in collaboration with eating disorder charity *beat*, one youngster commented: 'They're pretty and because of that they might be able to run really fast and like they're good at like reading and writing and they're good at all kind of things.' Girls who are overweight or less attractive were viewed as more likely to be unhappy or lonely.

Those who lived in London were the most aware and the most critical of their own bodies. Other factors the girls mentioned as important included families that had commented about appearance or having friends who had been singled out for their weight.

The biggest influence on the girls' awareness was people around them rather than magazines and television: positive comments from families and friends, coupled with reminders that looks aren't everything, were most likely to counter negative thoughts on body image.

After reading these results, in 2007 Girlguiding UK and *beat* formed a self-esteem youth panel which called for more experts to be invited into schools and for all adults to remember that their comments count.

Teenage
mental health:
Girls shout out!
A generation under stress?

A research report by
Girlguiding UK

Girlguiding UK

Too much too young

Pressure to grow up too fast has taken a toll on the mental health of teenage girls. That was the finding of the third *Girls Shout Out!* survey, which concentrated on the emotional well-being of 10–14-year-olds. The survey found that early sexualisation, materialism and boredom had led to mental health issues in many.

Subtitled *A Generation Under Stress?*, the survey found that self-harming was regarded as normal behaviour; sexual and material 'ideals' led to increased bullying; boredom was linked with aggressive behaviour; and that supportive friends and family are the most important factor in helping girls avoid mental health problems.

In focus groups held around the UK, Guides explained that pressure to grow up before they felt ready was among the greatest influences on their mental well-being. Many felt compelled to wear clothes that made them look older, had received sexual advances from boys and felt that magazines and websites that send the wrong messages regarding

weight loss and make-up and even encourage plastic surgery were damaging.

Two-fifths admitted they felt worse about themselves after seeing images of models, pop stars and actresses. One-third knew someone who had suffered from an eating disorder while two-fifths knew someone who self-harmed. Many felt self-harm was an acceptable part of growing up, and one girl linked it to a particular social group: 'One of my best mates, she was an Emo, and me and Charlie stopped her because she kept cutting her wrist . . . She was doing it to fit in with the Emos.'

Pressure to have the latest fashion or gadget also caused problems, with a quarter feeling bad about themselves because of material expectations. Girls also admitted that anti-social behaviour was often triggered by boredom, with one girl telling the pollsters: 'If I get bored then I start becoming really aggressive.' Half of those polled said they find anger difficult to deal with and 28 per cent said they were often worried and felt that no one understood them.

Dr Andrew McCulloch, Chief Executive of the Mental Health Foundation, which collaborated on the survey, commented: 'Girls and young women are being forced to grow up at an unnatural pace in a society that we, as adults, have created and it's damaging their emotional well-being. We have a responsibility to put this right – we must tackle head on the difficulties that the younger generation are facing.'

Active citizenship

Domestic violence, knife crime and bullying should be top of today's political agenda, according to Senior Section members. The fourth *Girls Shout Out!* survey, published in December 2008, found that girls wanted more young people to be involved in politics and called for a Youth Green Paper to ensure that prospective candidate shortlists included at least one person under 25.

Surprisingly, the survey, which questioned 1,000 girls between 14 and 25, found that even among guiding members, who traditionally work within their community and the voluntary sector, young people feel distanced from politics and believe their voice is not being heard by politicians.

Although 96 per cent of the girls questioned engage in volunteering and spend an average of just over two hours a week helping others, less than half of those have any involvement with politics (45 per cent) and those who do commit only 25 minutes a week, on average. They simply do not see politics as a necessary inclusion in their roles as useful citizens. As one put it: 'When I think about being an active citizen, I don't think about politics. I volunteer – but politics just never occurred to me.'

One-third of the girls thought that they were less interested in politics than their parents' generation and a fifth are deterred by their belief that politics is not worth the effort. A considerable number seemed to be put off by the lack of young and female MPs in Parliament. 'When one of the most high-profile women in politics feels she has to resign to spend more time with her family, it makes women feel that they can't do both,' said one girl.

Over half the girls believed that stopping domestic violence against women and children was the most important issue today. Tackling knife crime and gangs was second (46 per cent), followed by standing up against bullying (39 per cent) and making sure women have the same career opportunities

as men (36 per cent). The problems facing young women in society also featured: 33 per cent named pressure to have sex before they are ready as an issue, 27 per cent called for a ban on airbrushing models' pictures and a quarter called for equal pay.

Girlguiding UK's Chief Executive, Denise King, said:

Girls in guiding are committed volunteers, who care deeply about a wide range of issues. But they are sceptical about whether politics can help make a difference. As we approach the next election, the first time many of our members will be able to vote, it is vital that everyone who cares about giving young people a voice listens carefully to their recommendations.

In War and Peace

As 15 German Guides bade farewell to their English hosts in April 1914, they chatted excitedly about the return visit, when the UK Guides would go to Germany. The date was set for the following August, and the youngsters, who had become firm friends during their week of sightseeing in London, were eager to stay in touch. However, barely four months later, the two countries were at war and the return visit had become an impossibility.

One Guide from Leeds, who happened to be in Germany as the First World War broke out, was kept prisoner for eight weeks, but she kept her spirits up by making a Union Flag for her Second Class test!

While in Berlin, the Guide had met the German group leader, Fraulein Von Der Becke, and reported her great sorrow that a postponement of the return visit had been necessary. The hand of friendship was extended further by the *Girl Guides' Gazette*, whose editorial on the political situation read: 'Before the war broke out many of us had good friends amongst the German people – peace lovers to whom this fearful outbreak must have caused as much distress as it has to us. We can only hope that we shall soon be able to meet them again in happier circumstances. We must not think unkindly of them just because they happen to belong to a nation with whom we are at war …'

On the other side of the conflict, German Guides were also showing their compassion for the 'enemy'. One British soldier, captured in 1914 and held in prison camps, reported a touching meeting in 1916 as he worked felling trees on a country estate: a girl who lived on the next estate stopped her horse and spoke to him in English, asking him if he received parcels from home and whether he would like to borrow some books. For several years she had been a Girl Guide at an English boarding school in West Malvern and, as the soldier recalled, 'She didn't seem a stranger from the first. I had met with nothing but harshness for the whole time I had been in Germany, but she was kinder than anybody I had met anywhere.' She was brave, too, continuing to supply her English friend with books long after she was warned off by local police.

The First World War brought some benefit to the movement, since it did much to dispel the hostility suffered by the early Guides. The skills that were dismissed as 'unseemly' and 'boyish' by critics of the movement proved suddenly very useful, and with more and more young men being called up to fight, the young ladies of the Guides were ready to step into the breach.

War broke out on 4 August 1914, and only a day later an emergency meeting at Guide Headquarters was called to discuss the role the girls could play during the dark days ahead. Guides had already been showing up at the offices to volunteer their help, and it was decided this willingness to be of service should be given direction. A letter was published later that month in the *Girl Guides' Gazette*, urging Guides to carry out the duties 'for which they have been organised and trained'. The letter went on to say, 'The

LEFT: Guides collecting waste paper during the First World War

RIGHT:
Egg certificate

FAR RIGHT:
Guides making
swabs at their local
hospital during the
First World War

THE
NATIONAL
· EGG ·
COLLECTION
Patron
H.M. QUEEN ALEXANDRA

1914 – 1919
Certificate of Honour

Presented
To Mrs. Newton
Assist. P. Moll...

In recognition of valuable services rendered in the
collection of Eggs for the Wounded Soldiers and Sailors in
The Great War.

Signed. Chairman
Secretary

Guides' duties would be non-military,' and asked for the girls to offer their services to Red Cross detachments, hospitals, crèches, soup kitchens and convalescent homes. They were also urged to become cycle messengers and childminders, to help with home nursing as well as lending their talents to cooking, needlework and laundry work for hospitals and other institutions.

The following issue contained a letter from Olave Baden-Powell which suggested that 'the Guides should make or collect warm clothes for the children of poor families affected by the war, should visit and cheer up people who are ill, should make and distribute nourishing soup, and should knit socks and comforters for the Boy Scouts who are on duty helping the coast-guards'.

The girls also grew food on allotments and joined the National Egg Collection scheme, which provided freshly laid eggs for British soldiers wounded in France.

A letter from the secretary of the egg scheme was published in the *Gazette* in 1917, explaining:

Scouts and Guides have done excellent work in the past by going round to their neighbours and getting promises of a few eggs a week, which they then collect at Club Headquarters and pack and send off. We want them to keep on with this valuable service as much as possible.

RIGHT:
Girl Guides making themselves of practical use

In May 1915, the following notice appeared in the *Gazette*:

The War Service badge will be granted on the recommendation of a captain, and approved by the Commissioner, to all Guides and Guide officers who have performed (or shall perform by the end of the war) alternatively:

a. Not fewer than twenty-one days' special service for Hospitals, Nursing Institutions and other Public Departments, or Societies or Girl Guide Hostels. This service must be at the request of some competent authority and must be carried out for at least three hours a day; or

b. Not fewer than fifteen articles personally made to include four pairs of socks, four pairs of mittens, two shirts, one pyjama suit, one child's garment, one woman's garment, one belt and one bed jacket. Knitting and needlework already done for Sailors, Soldiers, Sea Scouts, Belgian Refugees, Hospitals etc may count;

c. For twenty-one days' work, not necessarily consecutive, in connection with recognised firms working directly for the government in connection with the war, or in connection with 'War Service for Women' initiated by the Government Labour Exchanges, in such work as farm work, dairy work, market gardening, poultry farming, light machinery for armaments, clothing machining, brush making etc.

It was later decided that paid work did not count for the badge, making it harder for the many teenagers who left school and went to work aged 14 and 15. Work on allotments and in gardens, to increase the food yield of the nation, was added, as was the making of 200 'treasure bags'. The badge was awarded on a yearly basis, so many Guides achieved more than one. In all 1,400 service badges were awarded.

In addition to these duties, the Association suggested that Guides could volunteer to be messengers for government departments and organisations. The Guides gained such a good reputation for doing this that they were approached by Marconi Wireless and Telegraph Company, which needed messengers to carry highly confidential information.

Winifred Birt-Kempton of the All Saints Guide Company in Lambeth was given the important task of relaying private messages from Marconi to Admiral Lord Fisher at the Admiralty. In gratitude, Marconi presented her with a special badge.

The movement as a whole also gifted a recreation hut for the soldiers in France. The Scouts had already donated one, and Olave Baden-Powell, who was working in the canteen in this hut, was struck by the morale boost it gave the men. She suggested the Guides raise 10,000 shillings (£500) for another in a different camp. The money flowed in from all parts of the Empire, and by the time the fund closed the sum was almost five times the target, at £2,348. The hut was

RIGHT: The hut in France which Guides raised funds for

BE PREPARED

To The 1st Llanishen Company

With cordial thanks for what you have done for the Soldiers' Hut Fund.

Robert Baden-Powell
Olave Baden-Powell

RIGHT: The badge presented by Marconi to Winifred Birt-Kempton

Guide hero

When North Street School in Poplar, London, was bombed in June 1917, the Captain of the 3rd Poplar Company was on duty nearby. She immediately rushed to help, pulling children – dead and alive – out of the rubble. She personally carried out four dead and several survivors. Of the 18 children who died, only two were over the age of five.

As long as life lasts I shall remember with admiration and pride the perfect self-control of those eighty daughters of England. Their behaviour was superb. The rule that a Girl Guide must smile under difficulties was kept absolutely through moments fraught with peril.

Letter from a Folkestone clergyman who presided over a religious service in 1917, during an air raid and while nearby buildings were being heavily bombed.

built at a large army centre in France, opening in April 1917. The fund also allowed for several extensions later in the year, including a billiard room, a quiet room for letter-writing and accommodation for the Guiders who were working in the canteen. The balance of the money went towards buying an ambulance, presented by HRH The Princess Mary to General Sir Francis Lloyd at a ceremony in the grounds of Buckingham Palace attended by 44 Guides. The vehicle proved a welcome addition to the military fleet, ferrying wounded soldiers from the front for a year and a half.

Peace at last

On 11 November 1918 the war ended; and over the next year the Guides contributed as much to the peace celebrations as they had to the war effort. The British government had been highly impressed with the Guides who had helped ministerial departments throughout the conflict, and, as preparations were made for the peace treaty in Paris, the request was made for eight Rangers and two Guiders to accompany the British delegation and act as messengers. They left in December, and in 1919 were joined by seven more. The work was highly confidential and the delegates placed their utmost trust in the girls.

CONGRES DE LA PAIX
VERSAILLES 1919
———
SÉANCE DE LA SIGNATURE DU TRAITÉ DE PAIX
DANS LA
GALERIE DES GLACES DU CHÂTEAU DE VERSAILLES
LE 28 JUIN 1919
———
M_____   N° ▓▓▓▓▓
———
Carte donnant accès à la TERRASSE du Château
à partir de 3 heures.
ENTRÉE : GRILLE DES RÉSERVOIRS.

ABOVE:
A pass to witness
the signing of
the Versailles
peace treaty

While working hard, it seems, the Paris party also played hard – in the nicest possible way. An employee of the Majestic Hotel, on the top floor of which the girls stayed, received several complaints about their playing games along the passage, disturbing the guests below.

RIGHT: Guides
and Guiders
who acted as
messengers
at the peace
conference in
Versailles in 1919

Many of the girls were rewarded for their efforts when they were given a place on the terrace at the Palace of Versailles to witness the historic signing of the peace treaty on 28 June 1919.

Two further events involved the Guides in the celebrations – a Royal Garden Party for the chosen few and a peace rally for many. The 50 Guides chosen for their outstanding war work travelled from all over the UK to join 50 Scouts at Buckingham Palace for a party hosted by King George V and Queen Mary. The girls formed a pathway for the Royal couple, who stopped and chatted to them and asked about their badges. Robert and Olave Baden-Powell then joined them all for tea.

In November, nearly a year after the Armistice, a great peace rally was held at the Royal Albert Hall in London.

It was attended by the Baden-Powells and 13,000 Guides from all over the UK. As Princess Mary entered the auditorium, the throng simultaneously turned towards the Royal Box to salute her, before hearing addresses from various speakers including Robert and Olave Baden-Powell. Robert Baden-Powell told them that small unselfish deeds could lead to greater peace and understanding.

'It is a glorious thought, if you can only grasp it, that each one of you can go further and take a valuable part in this great work for God, for your King, and for your country. There is no doubt at all that you can do this. The only question is – Will you do it?' The gathered Guides answered in unison: 'We will!' Robert Baden-Powell ended his speech by telling them: 'I want you to feel when you go out from this hall that the occasion is not over – it is only the beginning!'

Then the standard bearers, representing the countries where Guides existed, moved in procession to the centre of the stage and saluted the Union Flag before dedicating their colours to the service of mankind.

A Bronze for Bravery

Olga Drahonowska-Małkowska was the founder of the Girl Guides in Poland. Together with her husband, Andrzej Małkowski, she was also instrumental in the foundation of the Polish Scouts. In the summer of 1914 she organised the first national camp, which girls from the Russian- and German-controlled regions of Poland used false passports to attend. These were dangerous times, and even in the friendly atmosphere of the camp a young spy was caught as she rifled through Olga's tent in an attempt to find the real names of the Guides. When they were half-way through the camp they received a message from the Polish Secret Military Police, some of whom were the Guides' brothers, informing them that war had been declared and that the borders were closed. The girls found accommodation in the town of Zakopane, where Olga looked after them and set up a café to earn their keep. Throughout the first year of the war Olga's large company of 300 girls paraded each morning in the central square and took on a huge number of tasks, including the running of a children's home, helping with the harvest and setting up a hospital.

Forced to leave Zakopane in 1915, Olga returned in 1921 to resume her activities with the Polish Guides. She led the Polish contingent to Foxlease in 1924 and a year later set up a school and orphanage, run on the principles of Scouts and Guides. In 1932 she attended the World Conference in Bucz, where she was elected to the World Committee.

When the Second World War broke out Olga decided to take two orphans and a group of Rangers who had been running the school to a neutral country; but the train on which they travelled came under frequent fire from planes with machine guns. She maintained after the event that the training the Rangers had received saved their lives, since they instantly obeyed her order to scatter, making them less easy targets than those passengers who huddled together.

The group made it to a safe orphanage in Romania, where the Rangers offered to stay to help. Olga made her way to the UK, where she arrived at Headquarters; her tale of the terror and bravery of the Polish Guides was published in *The Guider* the following month. The article ended with a letter from Olga to the British Guides which began, 'I was deeply touched by your kindness and eager readiness to give help to our Polish refugees.' The letter concluded: 'Difficult times may be ahead and we have to be ready for them. But we shall be ready for the time when war will end and we will have to put all our strength and courage and will into the building of a new world, where the horrors of these days will never be repeated again.'

In November 1939 Queen Elizabeth awarded Olga the Bronze Cross at Guide Headquarters. 'I give you this for the Guides of Poland,' she said. 'But no one has earned it more than you.'

Olga went on to open a school for Polish refugees in Devon and was instantly flooded with gifts of woollen blankets, clothing, toys, books and stationery from sympathetic Guides all over the UK.

RIGHT: Queen Elizabeth speaks to Madame Malkowska after presenting her with the Bronze Cross for gallantry

The Second World War

In September 1939 when the news crackled over the radio that Britain was once more at war the Guides were immediately galvanised into action. In the first instance, there were gas masks to be distributed, since the threat of poisoned gas was the biggest fear. Secondly, as the children started to be evacuated from the major cities, along with mothers with young babies, the Guides were on hand to help. They acted as messengers for the officials dealing with the ordeal, met the evacuees from trains, reassured frightened and homesick tots, carried luggage, made tea and warmed babies' bottles. In one house on the south coast, which was to provide shelter for 50 girls from London, they cleaned the house from top to bottom and then knocked on doors to collect food, cooking utensils, bedding and black-out material for the curtains.

'I have never had much to do with girls,' wrote a billeting officer. 'But I find these Guides most level-headed and sensible. When you ask them to do a job they *do* get on with it, and they do it thoroughly.'

For those Guides who were themselves among the evacuees, there was a warm welcome as packs in rural areas made it their duty to seek out fellow members and take them along to meetings.

The 'Make Do and Mend' campaign that was to be run by the government later in the war was preceded by the Guides' own salvage initiative, 'Save All Supplies', launched in December 1939. The aim was threefold: to reuse and recycle items usually regarded as junk; increase food supplies; and to raise money through the sale of unwanted items. Empty shops and garden sheds became 'dumps', and Guides wheeled carts around the neighbourhood collecting waste paper, old jam jars, batteries and even bones, which could be used by the munitions factories to make glycerine. They fixed old toys for evacuees, washed and mended discarded clothes and collected wood and even fir cones for fuel. In 1941, when the RAF desperately needed 15,000 cotton reels for a secret job, they came to the Guides. Within a week they had 42,000 reels.

LEFT: Guides from Bishop's Stortford lay on tea for evacuees and mothers in 1940

LEFT: HRH The Princess Elizabeth and HRH Princess Margaret release a pigeon from Windsor to fly to the Chief Guide on 20 February 1943

Thinking Day message

Princess Elizabeth sent her own Thinking Day message by pigeon:
The winged message I send you all brings greetings and good wishes from my sister and myself with our sense of pride and thankfulness that Guides everywhere are taking their share in the great fight against evil.

Growing vegetables was another way in which the Guides proved useful. With food supply lines cut, and rationing kicking in, any additional food source was very welcome, and so gardens and allotments were dug and sowed by Guides everywhere. As well as feeding the local community, the girls sold some of the produce to raise money for the Red Cross and other causes.

In 1940 it was all hands on deck for the Rangers when the Home Emergency Scheme was devised. This was an intensive training scheme open to all Rangers of 15 years and above who were not already engaged in service and were prepared to sacrifice time and energy to train for specialist work.

In the same year a new money-raising idea was put forward in *The Guider*. In order to buy two air ambulances for the British forces, Brownies, Guides and Rangers were asked to sacrifice half a day's salary or a proportion of their pocket money. The scheme, which was named Guide Gift Week, set the ambitious target of £20,000 and was launched with a letter from the Chief Commissioner Mrs St John Atkinson, who asked 'Will you give half a day to your country?' Amazingly, the target was not only reached but more than doubled, with a total pot of over £50,000.

Other fundraising initiatives included the Baden-Powell Memorial Fund, launched after Lord Baden-Powell's death in 1941, which raised £100,000; and Target Months, which raised money for special projects such as rocket lifelines and dinghies for airmen. One had the girls raising £26,000 to equip and maintain carrier pigeons for the army. The Army Pigeon Service was so impressed that it arranged to fly a pigeon from each county to Guide Headquarters with a Thinking Day message for the Chief Guide.

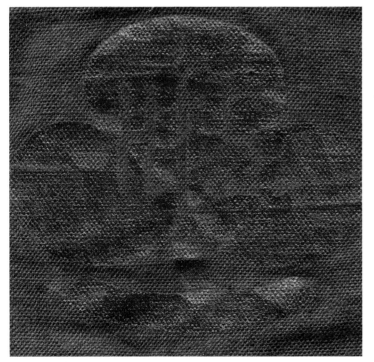

FAR LEFT: Home Emergency Service armband

LEFT: The Guide Gift Scheme, Bournemouth 1940

Second World War Service badge

Once again a War Service badge was introduced, with similar objectives to that issued in the First World War.

The badge was awarded on completion of 96 hours of voluntary war service within any 12 months. In the case of time spent 'on call' for First-Aid Posts and similar jobs, 144 hours had to be completed instead of 96. The badge showed a crown, with a separate date-strip for each year worn underneath.

Any Guide could qualify for the War Service badge, but it would not be awarded until the girl had passed her Second Class test.

The work had to be undertaken with the approval of the local Guider or Commissioner and signed for by the authority under whom she had worked.

Prepared for peace

Long before the end of the war was in sight, the Guides were living up to their motto and were determined to 'Be Prepared'. Anticipating the devastation that would be left behind in Europe, many were asking what they should be doing to help rebuild the lives of others when the conflict was over.

In 1941 a letter from Rose Kerr appeared in *The Guider* appealing for an 'army of peace'. 'Whatever happens Europe will be left weak and exhausted and will need and army of peace, an army mainly composed of women who will be in the front line, ready to bind the wounds and to heal the infirmities of those who have suffered.' Thus, the Guide International Service (GIS) came into

being, comprising of older Rangers and Guiders who were to undertake a tough training programme. Only the toughest were chosen, and to prepare for the hardships ahead, they camped outside in winter with little food, practised pulling heavy loads over rough terrain and learned the languages of the affected countries. They each took a driving test, which included jumping out of and back into a moving vehicle, and money was raised for equipment.

The first team left for Egypt in 1944 to work in a camp for Greek refugees, and others followed to many parts of Europe and Malaya to work in displaced person camps, distributing food and helping homeless families.

A team of the GIS working in Holland in July 1945 was requested to be present at Belsen in Germany. Among the first to enter the notorious concentration camp, they helped in the camp clinic and the children's hospital, took English classes and worked out rates of pay for the displaced workers. After four months they moved on to Gebhardshagen to assist in repatriating Polish displaced persons.

The work in Germany continued until 1952, when the German Government took over. It requested, however, that Commissioner Gwen Hesketh stay until April to provide 'a great example to all welfare workers'. She agreed, remaining with fellow Australian Peg Edmondson and English GIS member Sue Ryder (who was to go on to set up homes for the survivors of concentration camps as well as a charity to help those suffering from debilitating diseases). At the end of 1952 the section was closed down.

LEFT: Heroines in training: GIS members dismantle their trek cart and carry the parts through difficult country

RIGHT: A group of refugee children in their barrack home in a camp near Lubeck in Germany, 1951

The stoutest hearts

As the Second World War raged in Europe, in January 1942 a young military nurse and a handsome doctor were celebrating their wedding in Singapore. Four days later the country was invaded by the Japanese – and it was to be three years before Elizabeth Ennis saw husband Jack again.

British prisoners of war were interned at Changi Prison in February 1942, and as an antidote to the appalling conditions in the camp Mrs Ennis wasted no time in setting up a Guide company. By the end of the year there were 20 members, who met in the corner of the exercise yard once a week. At one meeting, the girls discovered that their beloved captain would soon be celebrating a birthday and so they set about making her a quilt as a present. Despite the lack of clothes and fabric available, every tiny scrap of material and piece of thread was saved and used to create hexagonal flowers for the gift, which is known as 'Grandmother's Garden Quilt'. Each Guide stitched her name to the pieces she had made and the finished product, gratefully accepted by Mrs Ennis, became the inspiration for many more, now known as the 'Changi Quilts'.

As most of the Guides were British, Mrs Ennis, who survived the war to be reunited with her husband, wished the quilt to return to the UK after her death; in 2006 it was presented to the Imperial War Museum by two of the former Guides from the Changi Prison Company. This is just one example of the bravery and fortitude of Guides in internment camps all over the world.

Throughout the Second World War, girls from Britain and the Allied countries formed companies in appalling conditions, where food and clothing was scarce and illness rife. Guiding gave them a focus, a social outlet and a way to take their minds off their everyday existence.

One such group was caught in the middle of the war between China and Japan even before the war in Europe had begun. In 1938, in North China, the China Island Mission School was captured by Japanese forces and put under their protection. The 1st Chefoo Brownies already had six groups – the Sprites, Elves, Imps, Kelpies, Pixies and Fairies – who continued to meet every Tuesday afternoon; there were also Guides and Ranger Companies.

After the bombing of Pearl Harbor, signalling Japan's entry into the wider conflict of the Second World War, civilians from the Allied Nations living in China were placed under house arrest; yet, amazingly, the units still managed to meet.

In the autumn of 1942, China's Britons were moved to Wei-hsien Concentration Camp, where the Brownie,

Guide and Ranger meetings provided a great source of comfort in their bleak surroundings.

Another unit was started by Guider Mrs Lawless in this camp, where 1,800 British, American, Dutch and Belgian prisoners were held. In an account written in 1943, an American internee wrote, 'Mrs Lawless is heart and soul in this fine work, and is trying to make these days at the Wei-hsien concentration camp days the girls will never forget, not because of what it cost them so much as what it gave them in a glorious spirit of adventurous living and service.'

Sadly, Mrs Lawless, who kept the spirits of the camp's children high during their internment, did not live to see them freed, dying just two days before the arrival of the Allied Forces.

RIGHT: A page from the logbook of the 1st Chefoo Brownie Pack, November 1942

THIS IS THE SUN
THAT RIPENS THE FRUITS
THAT NOURISH THE BIRDS
THAT NEST IN THE TREES
THAT GIVE SHADE TO THE FLOWERS
THAT BLOOM IN THE COUNTRY THAT GOD MADE

Friday Nov. 21st

This week's Competition
2 points for the best story explaining this picture.

11. a m

They all say I'm a good-looking fellow. Who am I?

Good work is being done by our Brownies in the Concentration Camp

KELPIES   ELVES   IMPS
C.FRASER   E.MARTIN   J.BRUCE
D.FRASER   B.STRANGE   E.GRAHAM
B.PATCHETT   F.HOUGHTON   J.GOODWIN
E.EDWARDS   J.HOUGHTON?   J.BEVAN
D.KNIGHT   A.NORDMO   J.THOMPSON
                 K.PHILLIPS   M.TAYLOR

Squirrel acting Brown Owl in Pack. Concentration Rhoda Jean is her helper.
Meetings Tuesday.

Building a Base

S.O.S.
"We're Short Of Stuff"

JUST as a child grows out of its clothes, Guiding has for some time been growing out of all efforts to house its organising staff. The Guides have now definitely out-grown the building they have shared for so long with their brother Scouts, and the exciting moment has arrived when they are to have a separate Headquarters building of their own.

The site is found; a long building lease has been arranged; plans are ready. Now comes the task of building, and this is where we—the Commissioners, Guiders, Rangers, Guides and Brownies—come in. If it is to be our own Headquarters, then we must help build it. True, we might appeal in the public Press for funds, but, would it then be our OWN Headquarters? What about that little clause in the Book of Rules to which we have clung with such pride and tenacity for so long. . . . "money should be earned and not solicited!" Are we to go back on that now? We are sure your answer would be "Never! as long as Guides are strong enough to carry their own load." And we ARE strong enough if the will is there. Were it not so, the plans would never have been made, nor this appeal sent out.

IT WILL TAKE £74,500 TO BUILD AND FURNISH OUR HOUSE

Does that figure daunt you? It certainly does look rather big, but

THERE ARE OVER HALF A MILLION GUIDES TO HELP

In this great total are included Guides in the Overseas Dominions and in every part of the Empire. For, of course, we are asking them to contribute. The new Headquarters is to be theirs as much as ours; indeed, perhaps its value will seem even greater to Guides visiting the Motherland. We want them to have here a real home where they will always find a friendly welcome.

You will see that, like all difficulties, this problem of raising £74,500 does not look so formidable when it is squarely faced—indeed, the task already seems lighter. What we suggest is this—that every member of the Movement should contribute some part of the building material.

BUY A BRICK FOR HALF-A-CROWN

It will be possible for individual Guides to buy one brick, or companies, packs and districts may arrange to buy a piece of wall, part of the staircase, a window, door, pillar, etc. A complete price list will be found elsewhere. In order that those who come after us shall know how the Guides of 1929 helped to build the great Imperial Headquarters, a Roll will be made on which will be inscribed the names of all those who helped to build it. This Roll will be kept at Headquarters, but companies and packs who buy bricks, will receive a certificate designed by the Chief Scout himself for display in their own Club room.

Should there, by any chance, be friends of the Movement within it or without, who would undertake to provide one room in the new building completely equipped, £500 upwards would cover the cost of this, and the room would be named after the person or locality providing it, or by any other name suggested by the donor.

Let us all build together and look forward to seeing this splendid new building rising before our eyes as the result of our own efforts.

The Girl Guides Association
25 Buckingham Palace Road
London, S.W.1

THIS IS THE HOUSE THE GUIDES BUILT

Deep in the heart of London, facing the splendour of Buckingham Palace, sits Commonwealth Headquarters and the home of Girlguiding UK. Fittingly close to the home of the Royal family, who have given the movement so much patronage over the years, its very existence is proof that girl power can build something wonderful – literally brick by brick.

In its infancy, the Girl Guide movement and the Sea Scouts shared space in 116 Victoria Street. In the autumn of 1916, however, a fire in the building, caused by a fused wire, burnt their office out and damaged all the stock kept there.

Suddenly the Guides had to look for a new home, which they found at 76 Victoria Street. Happy, as always, to muck in, the four staff loaded the office effects on to two barrows borrowed from a friend of the cleaner and carted them off down the road. In the new premises the kitchen was used to store badges, emblems and the like, while the files were stored in a bath. Unfortunately, no one noticed the dripping tap and so, over the months, some of the letters and documents were reduced to a sodden mass!

Four years on, the staff was on the move once again, to 25 Buckingham Palace Road, a few doors down from the current building. The offices belonged to the Scouts, and although the Guides were grateful for the space offered, it soon proved too small for their requirements. They needed to house their tailoring department and shops, and so they leased two small units at numbers 17 and 19. As the Executive Committee cast around for suitable premises for the expanding movement, the perfect solution presented itself. In 1929, when the leases on the shops expired and notice was given that they were to be pulled down, the committee decided it would buy part of the plot and build a structure big enough to house all the departments of Guide Headquarters. The only snag was the cost – the huge sum of £74,500.

Undaunted, the committee turned to the best people to help in any situation – the girls themselves. Lord Baden-Powell launched the SOS Appeal – meaning Short of Stuff – and asked Guides and Brownies all over the world to contribute items to complete the project. The idea was that they would pay for specific materials.

FAR LEFT: The SOS Appeal to raise funds for the Headquarters

LEFT: Queen Mary enjoyed a cup of tea in the Headquarters' restaurant after the official opening on 20 March 1931

RIGHT: HM Queen Elizabeth opening the Heritage Centre in 1996

For instance, 2 shillings and sixpence bought a brick, 2 pounds and 10 shillings a staircase step, and between £5 and £50 provided a window or door. Each contributor was to have her name inscribed on a builders' roll and receive a certificate designed by Lord Baden-Powell. With their usual enthusiasm the girls set to work raising the money. One Brownie, whose Six Patrol mates all eagerly offered to donate pennies, turned up at the meeting with an actual brick, which was duly sent to HQ as a lucky charm.

One Australian company sent its donation with a specific request. The members asked that it be used for bricks to be built into the wall overlooking Buckingham Palace. They felt that they may never get to see the King themselves but

would be proud to think that he occasionally glanced up and spotted their very own bricks! As well as the money pouring in from the girls, there were large gifts from benefactors such as HRH The Princess Mary. The Carnegie Trust pledged £2,500 for the library, while Sir John Cargill, of Glasgow, gave £2,000 for the Council Chamber in memory of his wife, a keen supporter of the Guides.

The foundation stone for the building was laid by Princess Mary on 23 May 1930. Almost a year later, on 20 March, the Queen opened the Headquarters; Princess Mary, the President of the Guide Association, greeted her at the door as her hostess. The Queen toured the new home of the movement, visiting each room and meeting each head of

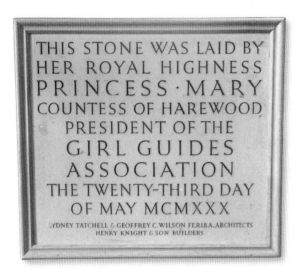

THIS STONE WAS LAID BY
HER ROYAL HIGHNESS
PRINCESS · MARY
COUNTESS OF HAREWOOD,
PRESIDENT OF THE
GIRL GUIDES
ASSOCIATION
THE TWENTY-THIRD DAY
OF MAY MCMXXX

SYDNEY TATCHELL & GEOFFREY C.WILSON F.F.R.I.B.A. ARCHITECTS
HENRY KNIGHT & SON BUILDERS

department, before a portrait of the Chief Scout by Simon Elwes was unveiled.

The handsome building is still occupied by the staff of Girlguiding UK and is visited by thousands of guiding members from around the world each year.

ICANDO London in a day

On 20 March 1939, Princesses Elizabeth and Margaret (a Guide and a Brownie, respectively) visited Guide Headquarters. They had come to see a new film and visit the camp shop, spending an exciting time among the tents and hiking equipment.

Fifty-seven years later to the day, the Queen accompanied by Princess Margaret returned to officially open the Guide Heritage Centre, unveiling a plaque under a large tent and trying out the interactive games.

The Heritage Centre changed its name to ICANDO in May 2003. It doubles as an activity centre and a starting point

for members visiting London. The centre presents a twofold challenge in *Seen London* and *Unseen London*. The first offers Patrols an organised trip around the capital, using a prepared pack and getting the girls to solve puzzles along the way. A digital camera is also provided to take snaps and the pictures can be taken home on a CD.

The second is an activity day based at the centre, where visiting units can experience London's diverse nature through exotic food tastings and can become a member of the Olympic Committee for a day. The lack of outdoor space does not stop the centre providing camping experience, as a huge indoor tent is able to sleep groups of up to 30. A word of warning though – lighting a campfire is not a good idea!

**TOP LEFT:
The plaque commemorating the foundation stone**

BELOW: A Brownie enjoys the newly refurbished ICANDO, 2009

Playing to Win

From managing directors and judges to award-winning actresses and famous politicians, many high-flying women regard their time in the Girl Guides as a contributory factor in their success.

Women in the Lead, a survey carried out by Girlguiding UK in 2007, targeted 250 inspirational UK figures and found that two-thirds of them had been a Brownie, Guide or Senior Section member. Of these, 73 per cent believed that guiding had directly contributed to their success. An overwhelming 87 per cent of respondents said that they learned to work as part of a team, 72 per cent that it helped them gain confidence and three-quarters that it made them more caring.

Instilling girls with useful skills, confidence and a sense of adventure was always the intention of Robert and Agnes Baden-Powell – a radical idea in the Edwardian era. Even as he penned *Scouting for Boys* the Chief Scout was voicing his admiration for heroic women.

Robert Baden-Powell said:

There have been women scouts of the nation, too, such as Grace Darling, who risked her life to save a shipwrecked crew; Florence Nightingale, who nursed sick soldiers in the Crimean War; Miss Kingsley, the African explorer; Lady Lugard in Africa and Alaska; and many devoted lady missionaries and nurses in all parts of our Empire. These have shown that women and girls as well as men and boys may well learn scouting when they are young and so be able to do useful work in the world as they grow older.

One hundred years on, when women can be found at all levels in all walks of life, guiding is still providing the tools to help them achieve their goals.

The current Chief Guide, Liz Burnley, says:

With over half a million members, Girlguiding UK is the largest organisation in the UK that provides a safe girl-only space for girls and young women. Since the organisation started out, our aim has always been to help girls and young women gain the confidence, skills and experiences necessary to broaden their horizons and reach for new goals. We prioritise leadership and management, assuming responsibility and building teams, taking the initiative, understanding rights and responsibilities, and caring for others – skills which our members can take into the rest of their lives, in their family, their work and their communities.

Baroness Shirley Williams, former Liberal Democrat Leader in the House of Lords:

Being a Brownie brought me new friends, an understanding of working in a team, and a sense of adventure – all very useful for a challenging public life; it also contributed to a lifelong love of the countryside, one of the pleasures of life at every age.

Dame Tanni Grey-Thompson, winner of six London Marathons and 16 Paralympic medals including 11 golds, and holder of over 30 world records:

Being involved in the guiding movement gave me confidence and helped me grow as a person. I had fun and learned about life without realising that I was doing it.

Diana Moran, the 'Green Goddess', fitness expert and journalist:

Being a Brownie and a Guide was an important and character-forming time of my life. The experience has stayed with me and today I apply many of the rules and principles learned in my youth. Even in my 60s I'm still in close touch with a handful of fellow Brownies and Guides who shared happy times with me. Many close friends regard me as 'an overgrown, enthusiastic Girl Guide'.

LEFT AND TOP: Dame Tanni Grey-Thompson as a Brownie and as she is today

RIGHT AND BOTTOM: Diana Moran then and now

Cherie Booth QC:

Guiding gave me the opportunity to have fun, make friends and do things I would never have done otherwise. My fondest memories are of singing Guide songs with other Guides on trips and somehow always being the one who fell into the stream and ended up going home in a motley collection of everyone else's clothes.

Clare Short, MP for Birmingham Ladywood and a former Labour Cabinet Minister:

I was in a pack in Birmingham, which met in a Baptist church in Hampstead Road. We had many adventures in the pack. We went camping although we didn't always stay overnight. We'd put up a tent and cook some beans, throw the lanyard around and so on. Once I went with a whole camp full of Guides to help the Life Guards, because it was by the sea. My friend Liz had her Lifesaving badge and I was her assistant, and I enjoyed it enormously.

We won a prize for having the tidiest tent and then, on the way back on the train, I got a prize for being one of the most popular guides – and I was absolutely astonished because I wasn't even in that troop! It was one of the most touching moments of my life, one of those things that comes from out of the blue and makes you feel wonderful.

The overwhelming thing I got from Guides is all the practical, sensible knowledge which is still useful today – how to deal with emergencies, how to conduct things, how to make and mend things. I think

it's nice to look after things, create things, fix things and go for walks and light fires.

When I first became an MP I received a letter from my Brown Owl, saying 'Congratulations. Now you see how we helped train and develop your talents.' She obviously thought it was because of what I did in the Brownies!

Laura Tenison MBE, founder of successful mail-order clothes firm JoJo Maman Bébé:

I was a good Girl Guide in that I liked the challenge of taking the badges, and I liked the fact that they involved doing different things each time to collect a new accolade. I did badges in the most obscure subjects – I even did one in identifying bird eggs! I loved that challenge and the fact that I had a weekly aim to achieve. It's always empowering to achieve things.

Emma Thompson, Oscar-winning actress:

Through organisations like the World Association of Girl Guides and Girl Scouts, girls and young women can gain the confidence to be equal partners and to make informed, responsible choices about their lives.

Roberta Bondar, space explorer, Canada:

For me Guides was extremely important. I took my Brownie wings that we got when we flew from Brownies to Girl Guides, into space with me. My first set of wings: you don't know how important that was to me.

Margaret Lester, Social Worker of the Year 1995:

Having left Guides at 14, I rejoined at 19 when I was at university because I wanted to be a social worker and this was a good way of gaining experience of working with children. I was asked to run a Guide unit in a colliery village in the north-east, where the Guides came either from the children's home or the council estate in the village. Most had never been out of the village, or been to the seaside, which was only five miles away and most had never been on holiday in the country. When we went to camp they were very excited to see sheep and lambs.

The fundamental values of guiding are about respect for others and their views, the need to listen to others, the development of girls as active citizens that gives them rights and responsibilities as a citizen. Our international aspect also gives us an opportunity to experience other cultures and lives. I will never forget being in South Africa when Mandela was freed and when so much was changing. It gave me insights into different lives.

Liz Carnell, founder of charity Bullying Online and winner of the Pride of Britain Special Award:

Being a Girl Guide gives you all the skills you need to help others and teaches you leadership.

Gold star

I was a Pixie Sixer in the Brownies and a Patrol Leader in the Guides. Friday night was Guide night and I enjoyed it so much that I was doing that as well as training for my running. I think guiding has taught me to appreciate the outdoors and that it's not all about materialistic things. It was a really good grounding. It taught me interesting ways of doing things and making things and, because we used to go to visit old people's homes and raise money for good causes, it made me more caring.

Olympic Gold Medallist Sally Gunnell was a Brownie and then a Girl Guide in Chigwell, Essex.

Other famous Guides:

Kaye Adams

Clare Balding

Baroness Virginia Bottomley

Edith Bowman

Sarah Brown

Rhona Cameron

Lady Hazel Cosgrove (Judge)

Annette Crosbie

Cat Deeley

Vanessa Feltz

Kirsty Gallacher

Lesley Garrett

Jennifer Harris (*The Times* Young Businesswoman of the Year 2005)

Dorothy Hodgkin

Dame Kelly Holmes

Hazel Irvine

Glenda Jackson

Ashley Jensen

Natasha Kaplinsky

Lulu

Davina McCall

Claire Rayner

Angela Rippon

J.K. Rowling

Helen Sharman

Lisa Stansfield

Sandi Toksvig

Jayne Torvill

Carol Vorderman

Kirsty Wark

Star Quality

LEFT: Girls get loud at the BIG GIG 2006

*Girl Guides get to do so many activities. I think it's
wonderful and I personally think that all children should have
something like that.* Alesha Dixon, BIG GIG 2006

Girls Aloud, Kate Nash, Rachel Stevens and Atomic
Kitten are among the fabulous acts to have played at
the Girlguiding UK popfest, the BIG GIG. The generous
organisers even let some boys into the girl-only space for
the event – providing they came with names as famous as
Mark Owen, McFly, Lemar and The Hoosiers!

October 2008 saw the tenth annual gig take place at
Birmingham's LG Arena, with headliners such as The
Saturdays, Sugababes and the appropriately dubbed
Scouting for Girls, who told the excited crowd 'We're your
band!' The show, hosted by TV hosts Sam and Mark, was
watched by 22,000 girls and young women, most of whom
were wearing flashing blue bunny ears.

'It is a great example of how Girlguiding UK's modern
*and relevant programme really does extend well beyond
badges,*' said Chief Guide Liz Burnley. '*The girls are
today involved in a hugely diverse range of activities,
like the BIG GIG.*'

The idea of making the BIG GIG a yearly date came
after two one-off events (one of which was a night
at the Millennium Dome in 2000, which proved
hugely popular with the girls). Geri Halliwell
brought her special brand of Girl Power to the
2001 event, the first to be named the BIG
GIG, and was joined by A1, Louise and
Liberty X. By 2003 the word had truly
spread and 11,000 tickets sold out in 90
minutes, making it the fastest-selling concert in
the history of Wembley Arena and prompting
a second date. In the
following two years the
BIG GIG moved
to Manchester
and Birmingham,
accommodating
an audience of over
22,000 at each, and for 2006 it
was back at Wembley with a similar crowd. A
year later, at the Manchester Evening News Arena,
the stars were joined by two unknowns, the winners
of the X-Factor-style competition for Guides,
Guiding Star.

A Guiding Star

As daylight dawned on Saturday, 13 October 2007 two talented but unknown singers tumbled out of bed with a huge feeling of excitement. As the winners of the Guiding Star talent competition, they had earned their place at the top of the bill at the BIG GIG. Later that day 14-year-old Izzy Stocchetti from Surrey and 18-year-old Samantha Laurilla from Hampshire would share the stage at Manchester's MEN Arena with top talents McFly, Natasha Bedingfield, Sophie Ellis-Bextor, Calvin Harris, The Hoosiers and Kate Nash.

For Izzy the event was the culmination of a dream that began with an X-Factor-style audition some months before. At the first audition Izzy met singer-songwriter Anna Neale and contacted her afterwards for a few lessons, which proved a big confidence booster: 'The lessons helped a lot and I developed so much throughout the competition.'

For the BIG GIG Izzy chose Delta Goodrem's 'Together We Are One' as her number, because of the appropriate lyrics. While the theme of working together and finding strength in unity was bound to resonate with the guiding family, one line in the chorus – 'Find your guiding inspiration in a place where dreams are made' – meant it was perfect.

'I thought that was really close to guiding and the rest of the lyrics really fitted the event,' says Izzy. 'It's all about bringing everyone together.'

On the night, the young singer got to meet Kate Nash, Natasha Bedingfield and The Hoosiers. When the time came to take to the stage and perform her big number in front of 27,000 people, Izzy loved every minute: 'It was fantastic. I wasn't nervous at all. I thought I was going to be but as soon as I came off I wanted to go straight back on stage and do it again. To see all the people with their flashing lights waving in the air was a real buzz. I thought "I love this!".'

And she may well be a name to look out for in the future. Izzy is already working on some demo tracks and hopes to make a career as a singer-songwriter. 'Guiding Star was fantastic for me and I will take it with me always,' she says. 'It's broadening what guiding can do and it shows that there is a lot of talent within the Guides. Everyone has different interests, and when you bring out those interests, people have a chance to shine.'

Girl Guides have long been the stars of radio and television, from *The Archers* to *The Darling Buds of May*. In the 1980s sitcom *To the Manor Born,* Audrey fforbes-Hamilton (played by Penelope Keith) was a County Commissioner and fought many a battle, with sidekick Marjory (Angela Thorne), on the Guides' behalf.

Brownies and Guides also featured in the 1999 film *Whatever Happened to Harold Smith?* starring Laura Fraser and Tom Courtenay; the 1987 Bisto advert, 'Now You're Home'; and in a 1976 episode of *Jim'll Fix It,* when a Brownie got her dearest wish – to meet the Chief Guide Lady Baden-Powell in person.

Pupils experiencing 1960s school life in *That'll Teach 'em* got to join a retro Guide unit, and in 1989 Sir Harry Secombe hosted a special guiding edition of *Highway* to celebrate the centenary of Olave Baden-Powell's birth.

The long-running children's show *Blue Peter* often featured the activities of members, and on one memorable occasion almost lost the studio in the process. The live show, aired in 1970, saw 100 Guides and Brownies seated around a mock campfire singing songs. When 'mock' became real, and smoke began to billow around the studio, the Guides continued their song as the BBC's fire squad put out the blaze. The following day a newspaper was scathing about the Guides' reaction, saying, 'We thought they should have jumped up and dealt with the fire.' The BBC replied that they were extremely glad the girls had done no such thing, and the following week showed a video of the dramatic moments, praising the calm, collected behaviour of the Guides.

British Guides Overseas

LEFT: 1st
Peninsular Guide
Company at the
British School in
Oporto in 1934

RIGHT: Salmiya
Brownies in Kuwait
in 2008

The wonders of modern technology have proved a particular boon for one very special section of guiding. The 3,847 members of Girlguiding BGIFC (British Guides in Foreign Countries) are UK nationals dotted around the world who carry out their guiding programme either in units or, if it is not possible for them to join in with girls from the local area, on their own. BGIFC units meet in 31 countries across Europe, the Middle East and Asia, and those out of reach of a unit can sign up as Lone Guides and meet up with other BGIFC members at camps every other year. Thanks to the Internet and email, BGIFC members can now keep in touch with the organisation and each other at the touch of a button, which makes working towards badges and taking part in projects a whole lot easier.

Imagine how much harder it must have been for the earliest troop, founded in 1911, who had to rely on letters and telegrams.

The 1st Peninsular Guide Company in Oporto was the first Guide unit in Portugal, registered in 1913. It was not until the 1930s that the Guias de Portugal (the national Association) emerged from the British Units. The 1st Oporto Brownie Guide Pack was formed in 1920, but sadly closed in 2005.

British Guide units soon followed in Argentina (1915), Hong Kong (1916, based at the Victoria British School), Malta (1918) and Uruguay (1924). The National Association of Uruguayan Guides was established 21 years later with a great deal of help from the BGIFC Leaders.

ABOVE: An English and Indian Guide company led by Mrs George John Carsie in India, during the First World War

In France, the 1st Paris Brownie Pack was formed and registered in 1920, to become the earliest French pack on record. And English-speaking girls at an army base in Vacaos, Mauritius, formed a troop in 1926.

Many of the BGIFC units were suspended during the Second World War because communication was so difficult, but the postwar years, when many military families were stationed in Europe, saw a boom in units.

The first Lone BGIFC Unit was formed in 1985 and in the same year girls travelled to Buckingham Palace from Belgium, Germany, the Netherlands and Oman to represent

BGIFC at the 75th Anniversary Celebrations. On 1 April 1986 important changes took place for BGIFC: formerly the responsibility of the Commissioner for Branch Associations, it was then reclassified as a 'Region' and given its own Commissioner, Advisers and Secretary.

For such a spread-out section of the Guiding movement, international camps are particularly exciting, allowing the members to meet in large groups and share in activities. Lone Guides, in particular, are encouraged to make contact with their nearest units as often as possible and to attend the BGIFC biennial camp in the UK.

Rachel, a Lone Guide in Spain

*I've lived in Spain for nearly ten years. I moved
here because of my Dad's job. I was a Rainbow in
the UK, then I left the guiding community, only to
return a few years later when I realised I could join
overseas. Being part of BGIFC has been amazing. I've
made some friends for life and learnt some amazing
skills that will never leave me. I have some brilliant
memories, and going to camp every two years has
been so fabulous! I keep in touch with other Guides
via email and post.*

Megan, a Lone Guide in Malta

*I was a seven-year-old Brownie when I moved
to Gozo, Malta, because of my father's work.
Unfortunately, at the time there were no Brownies
there so I became a Lone Brownie and, once I was
ten, a Lone Guide. Being a Lone is something that
you really benefit from. It's just like normal Guides
except that we do it by email and post. You learn
lots from the friends you make in different countries,
and learn about their countries. Completing your
badges is as easy as well, apart from a lot you have
to do yourself. Every two years BGIFC hold a camp
which I have attended three times running now, and I
intend to return because, honestly, those weeks have
been some of the most fun and best of my life.*

The First Lones

*Please say we may be Boy Scouts! We can run, jump,
climb a tree, track a man – in fact we can do anything!
But when you write, please don't say anything about
needlework, cooking, dusting or learning lessons,
because that is what mother says we must do, and
we hate it!*

This appeal from two eager sisters, in a letter to the Chief
Scout at the outset of the movement, brought to his
attention the many girls who were in remote rural areas

The Galleon

The BGIFC galleon badge is the equivalent of a County badge worn by other Guides. Its unusual design was chosen through a competition launched in 1926, and won by a Guide from the Île-de-France region of France.

The galleon sailing across the ocean represents the journey which has taken the Guide overseas, while the colours, red, white and blue represent the Union Flag. The red crusader cross on the sail is also a reference to the adventurous, crusading spirit of UK national guides who live and work abroad.

At first the metal badges were handpainted, with the name of the host country displayed on a scroll beneath the blue waves of the sea. As BGIFC became more widespread and demand rose, however, the galleon badges became mass produced.

RIGHT: Early handpainted BGIFC galleon badge

where a pack could not be formed. It was decided that they could become Lone Guides and pass their badges through correspondence. They were eventually grouped into companies, with a Captain keeping in touch through monthly letters and arranging the rare get-togethers. So the first Lone Guides were actually dotted around the UK rather than living abroad. The first Captain was Nesta Maude.

BGIFC in Germany

Germany has always boasted a thriving guiding community because of the many British servicemen and women stationed there throughout the 20th century, with the first unit forming at the garrison in Cologne, in 1921, for the daughters of British troops. A British Guides in Europe Division was formed in 1928 but, a year later, it was decided that Germany was large enough to become a separate Division.

A year after the end of the Second World War, moves were made to re-establish guiding for the families of British Forces personnel stationed in Germany, and the first President was appointed in 1948.

The movement continued to flourish among British communities in Germany for the next 50 years, with the majority of Leaders and members coming from the Forces' families. In 1993 army cutbacks meant that 1,000 members of BGIFC left the country and returned to the UK, where they were able to join local units. However, Germany is still one of the largest BGIFC Counties, with 11 Districts, 3 Senior Section units, 16 Guide units, 22 Brownie units and 19 Rainbow units, and it remains a stronghold of BGIFC.

The units are kept up to date with a county newsletter and the BGIFC units are looking to expand into new areas of Germany in the near future.

3

Girl Power

For 100 years, the Girl Guide movement has presented girls with challenges – whether it be earning a badge, helping out in times of need or raising funds for special projects. Each generation faces new and exciting ways of proving themselves and the goals they achieve have inevitably altered over the years. But no matter how times change one thing remains constant – a Guide always rises to a challenge.

In the year England celebrated its World Cup win, a group of determined guiding members scored a victory of their own. The summer of 1966 saw six girls break the female record for a cross-Channel relay swim when they swam from Cap Gris Nez in France to the Kent coast in 13 hours and 10 minutes.

The relay team was chosen from companies around the country and whipped into shape by a Miss B. Strutt, a physical education expert from Manchester University.

On the appointed day the first swimmer, Sally Rose, set out at 3.27am with the moon still up and a fog gathering on the water. Undeterred, the hearty Harlow Guide completed

FAR LEFT: Channel swimmers and the reserve team get a pep talk from their coach, Miss Strutt

LEFT: The team after the crossing

her first stint and declared that 'The water's comfortably warm. My hour went by very quickly. We're having a whale of a time!' The girls were accompanied by a boat, *The Accord*, carrying a doctor, the team leader, a reserve team of swimmers, two young signalmen from the Staffordshire regiment who handled ship-to-shore communications, two French Rangers and a press photographer as well as Miss Strutt, who shouted encouragement and instructions through a megaphone. There was also an observer from the Cross Channel Swimming Association on board to verify the time.The fog was so thick for the second and third swimmers, Susan Oley and Wendy Draper, that a fog light had to be used to keep them in sight, and swimmer number four, Karen Young, was forced to keep close to the boat as they passed through the busy traffic area of the Goodwins in poor visibility.

Swimmer number five, Christina White, had music from Radio Caroline to accompany her on her swim but was instructed to tread water for a few minutes after she found herself in the wash of large freighter. By 8.27am, the sixth

swimmer, Margaret Greenway, was on her first stint, and good progress was being made. In between stints the enterprising girls, who were on the separate boat *Fair Chance*, caught mackerel – and managed to bag 19 for their lunch.

During the morning, the girls received a message from Olave Baden-Powell which read: 'The very best of luck to all the girls. I shall be swimming with you all the way.'

A gale-force wind hit the swimmers as they neared their second stints, and Sally and Susan, swimming for the third time, completed the magnificent feat. Susan clambered on to the rocky beach near the cliffs of Dover, then presented a message, carried in plastic wrapping by the swimmers, from the French Guides to a waiting Kent Cadet.

Another message, from Miss Kelham Smith, Honorary Secretary of the Cross Channel Swimming Association, was also received: 'It's magnificent! You've done it – and you've done it in 13 hours, 10 minutes.'

Reaching new heights

Aiming for another entry in the record books, eight intrepid Girlguiding UK members headed for Mount Everest in September 2007. The aim was to achieve the highest altitude display tether of a hot air balloon.

From Lukla, at an altitude of 2,840m, the girls, aged between 18 and 33, trekked to Syangboche, at an altitude of just below 4,000m, carrying a huge hot air balloon bearing the Girlguiding UK insignia. Attempts to reach Everest Base Camp, however, were thwarted by a collapsed bridge, and the balloon was inflated at Syangboche instead. Jenni Smith, an Assistant Leader from Bournemouth, and Rachael Myers, a Leader from Berkshire, took it in turns to record their experiences in a journal.

7 September
We trekked to Namche Bazar, the starting point for treks to Base Camp. As we got to Namche, cloud descended. Some of the members of the group are feeling the effects of altitude sickness as we are now at 3,440m.

LEFT: The balloon is inflated in the record-breaking adventure

8 September
Today our attempt to tether the balloon was thwarted by thick cloud. We trekked up to the Everest View Hotel and were told that they hadn't seen Everest for five days! We compensated by singing songs and dancing like penguins.

9 September
We started at 3.30am. It was hard going – we trekked in the pitch black across rocky and uneven ground – but it was worth it. As we went around the corner of the hill, the panoramic view of Everest and its surrounding peaks took our breath away. But there was no time to waste as the mist moved in. We all helped and the balloon was inflated in no time – none of us could believe it. As soon as we deflated the balloon, the mist came in and we could no longer see three feet in front of us. We couldn't continue with our trek up to Everest Base Camp, so

we headed back to Lukla. We are tired but happy and determined to come back.

Despite their hampered attempt, the girls managed to break the record and, on their way home, they stopped at Kathmandu, where they celebrated by inflating the balloon again for 500 local Guides and Scouts.

The following year many of the original team, and some more willing volunteers, once more tackled the hallowed slopes in the name of charity.

In 2008, to raise awareness of Macmillan's World's Biggest Coffee Morning, 13 Senior Section members and Leaders from Girlguiding South West England decided to hold their own coffee morning 5,600m up near the Everest Base Camp. Beginning in Kathmandu on 1 September they trekked across vast areas of the Himalayas, reaching Base Camp on

FAR LEFT: The 2008 team reach 4,500m

LEFT: The Everest Challenge team with the balloon

RIGHT: Raising a cup at 5,600m in 2008

11 September. Lauren Calley was one of the girls who joined the second wave of adventurers.

I started Devon Junior Council, which is a group of girls within Guiding, who basically help at events and two of the girls asked if I fancied climbing up Everest so I thought, 'All right. Why not?'

We trained in the gym and did a lot of walking up on the moors as well, then we just had to keep our weight down and make sure that our BMI was all right. I was a bit nervous setting off but some of the girls that had been before came back as crew, so they could come along and tell us what to expect for the first bit. They reassured everybody.

The group took eight days to get to the base camp, with two rest days in between, and Lauren admits that some days it was hard to get motivated.

It was very tough. We'd get up in the morning and say, 'Oh no, not again!' but we always knew that we had Base Camp day to look forward to. I was with a good bunch of girls so everyone kept each other going. And, of course, I'd never have turned back!

The day the team arrived in base camp held mixed emotions for Lauren:

That day was such an important one, I think it was probably the scariest. There were snow and rocks and it was very hard work. You could see everything down below whereas before, because it had been covered by trees and boulders, it felt just like you were walking on a path.

When we got to base camp we had coffee and tea and took lots of photos, and some of the girls went for a walk. Then we had lunch and chat and went back down again. Some other climbers came up to the café where we stopped and they were saying, 'So you're the ones who are doing the coffee morning!' It was like everyone had heard about us by the time we got to the top, so that was quite cool.

It was amazing to be up there. I didn't want to go back down again. It wasn't something that I ever thought I'd do, so to get there was absolutely great.

While the Senior Section members were busy in the Himalayas, the Guides and Brownies at home were busy with Everest-themed fundraising events, including one coffee morning on a Plymouth ski slope!

Lauren, who is training to be a child nurse, says she would go back in a shot if she had the opportunity and believes the experience changed her outlook on life.

It just opens your eyes to everything and it makes you stop taking for granted the things that we have here. Being on a mountain, you see how other people are living and it makes you think about things more rather than going about day to day thinking it's the same as always.

I have conquered a lot of fears, I used to be afraid of heights but Guides has allowed me to conquer them by doing climbing and abseiling. My favourite experience is falling in to the river and getting soaked – it was so, so funny.

Rebecca, 2nd Liversedge Guides

Sailing into the record books

In the Tall Ships' Race in July 2007, the first fully female crew to take part on a Class A Tall Ship set sail from Liverpool in the *Lord Nelson*. Forty Senior Section members, some of them with special needs, joined eight professional sailors from the Jubilee Sailing Trust to sail into the history books. Abi Bubb was among the excited crew.

I saw the advert in the Guiding *magazine and I thought it sounded so exciting that I couldn't not apply. I'd been on dinghies on adventure holidays but I'd never sailed on anything as big as this. The majority of the crew hadn't sailed a boat that size before. We had a weekend on it a few months before when we learnt a bit, but we learnt most of it while we were sailing around.*

LEFT: Forty Senior Section members helped to make up the all-female crew of the *Lord Nelson*

RIGHT:
The *Lord Nelson*

The two-week race meant the women not only had to work together as a team but also had to learn with a lot of near strangers in a very tight space. 'I made a lot of lifelong friends, because we all got very close on the boat,' says Abi. 'Living and working together in such a small space, you have to get on.'

Although the girls failed to win the race, which ended in Maloy in Norway, they certainly enjoyed taking part:

We came last in our class because we got stuck with no wind near Skye, in Scotland, so we couldn't move for three days. There was talk of withdrawing from the race and giving up, which was depressing everyone more than the prospect of not winning the race. We couldn't give up so we kept going, but the wind was beyond our control. The most exciting moment for me was climbing the mast and getting to the platform way up there. Lots of people climbed to sort the sails out but I couldn't climb it until we were in Maloy, and it was an exhilarating feeling.

'I've got a lot of friends and some amazing memories to look back on,' says Abi. 'It's given me more confidence to go and do anything I want to do.'

Up and Active

RIGHT: Girlguiding
UK's Training and
Activity Centres

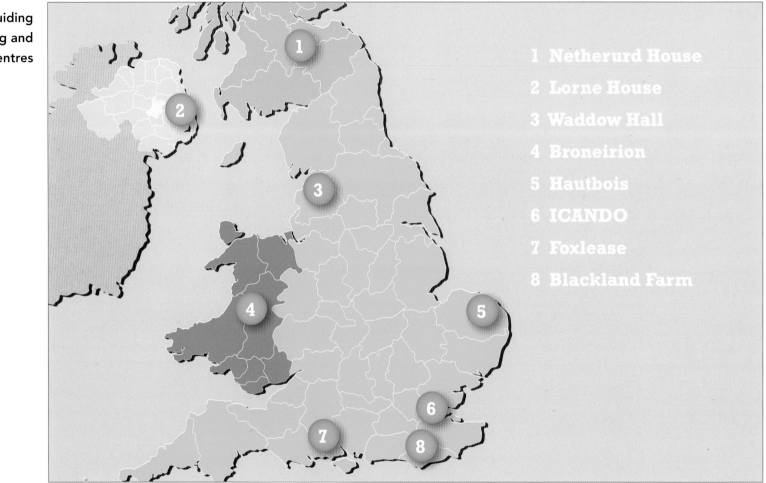

RIGHT: Girlguiding UK's Training and Activity Centres

1 **Netherurd House**

2 **Lorne House**

3 **Waddow Hall**

4 **Broneirion**

5 **Hautbois**

6 **ICANDO**

7 **Foxlease**

8 **Blackland Farm**

The activities enjoyed by the modern Guide have come a long way since the days of semaphore and sewing: at the Training and Activity Centres (TACs) dotted around the country, Leaders can train and enjoy leisure breaks while Rangers, Guides and Brownies can try everything from archery to assault courses and from kayaking to croquet. Increasingly the centres are providing activities for Rainbows too, with miniature climbing facilities, trampolines and play houses. The Guide Association's first centre was Foxlease, a generous gift from an American lady, Mrs Archbold Sanderson, which was opened in 1922 in Hampshire. Waddow Hall, bought to help Leaders in the North, followed five years later, and Training and Activity Centres were soon springing up in Wales, Scotland and Northern Ireland.

Waddow Hall

Waddow Hall is more than just a Training and Activity Centre – it nestles in the heart of Witch country and boasts its own resident ghost! The 17th-century manor overlooks the River Ribble in 178 acres of Lancashire landscape, and walks in the area could take in the historic market town of Clitheroe, the beautiful village of Waddington and Pendle Hill, famed for the famous witchcraft trials of 1612.

Visitors have also reported seeing the ghost of one Peg O'Nell, said to be a servant girl who argued frequently with her employers. Legend has it that her frustrated mistress sent her one night to fetch water from the well and, during the ensuing row, shouted, 'I hope you trip and break your neck.' That is what befell Peg, and she has apparently haunted Waddow Hall ever since.

LEFT: Waddow Hall nestles in huge and beautiful grounds

BELOW: The
climbing wall is
one of the most
popular activities

FAR LEFT: Girls can
learn archery

FAR RIGHT:
Girls enjoy the
woodlands at
Blackland Farm

However, the girls and Leaders who frequent the Hall and campsites and take part in the many activities are yet to be bothered by this most spirited of spirits.

Waddow Hall first came into the Guides' possession in 1927, when they took it for a trial period on the understanding they would buy it if a training centre in the North of England proved useful. After months of hard work, HRH The Princess Mary opened the centre on a wet day in October after passing down a drive lined with 1,500 volunteers. The response in the first year proved the need for a second training centre, giving those in the North the same facilities as those offered by Foxlease, and Waddow was duly purchased.

During the Second World War the building was lent to the Lancashire County Council, who used it as a children's hospital.

In 1952 Miss Christine Pilkington, of the first Waddow Committee, donated the Brownie Pack Holiday House, which was replaced in 2006 with a new adventure house used by Brownies, Guides and occasionally Rainbows on an overnight stay.

The stables and two farm cottages on the estate have also been furnished, so that they could be let out to members and their families. One is now being used to accommodate the increasing number of instructors employed to manage the exciting activity programme.

The campsites of Waddow play host to around 6,500 a year. The most popular activities include the crate-building challenge, archery and the assault course.

Down on the farm

Blackland Farm is an estate of 122 acres of land near the Ashdown Forest in the Sussex countryside. Bought in 1938 by a Mr A. R. Wagg on behalf of the Manor Charitable Trustees, it was leased to the Association until 1989 and then donated to it. Its name derives from the 16th-century iron industry centred in the Ashdown Forest which made it a 'black country'. The warden's house is the original farmhouse, parts of which date back 300 years.

It was the outbreak of the Second World War which really brought popularity to Blackland Farm. Because defence regulations insisted that all tents had to be camouflaged and pitched under trees, campers deserted the fields and for six years hundreds of Guides enjoyed their camping in the comparative peace of Blackland Woods.

With the return of peace the camps moved back into the fields, Nissen huts were purchased from the army and the estate began to develop into the Blackland we know today. In 1987 the woodland on the site was badly hit in a huge storm, and many of its beautiful old trees were felled. A replanting scheme was launched to replace the damaged trees, and the woodland is now restored to its former glory.

The woodland and grass areas have numerous campsites, both equipped and unequipped. There is also self-catering

Melissa, Katie and Beth, from 2nd Coxheath Guides visited Blackland Farm in December 2008.

We went abseiling and rock climbing, and I went on the bungee trampoline. We stayed in a cabin and we've been doing lots of badges in between. It's been brilliant.
Melissa

The activities are things you wouldn't normally do so if you can do it well then you can be proud of yourself. If it's something you're scared of, you can overcome that and enjoy yourself doing things that you couldn't do before.
Katie

We split into groups and some went abseiling, then we went on the zip wire and while we were on it we did positions like Superman or Tarzan, which was fun. Then we did all the low ropes together and a lot of people fell off so we had to work as a team to get across. It really helps working as a team.
Beth

indoor accommodation, and the range of activities is enough to keep any Guide or Leader happy. Archery, climbing and abseiling, canoeing and grass sledging are enjoyed all year round, a heated swimming pool means a dip can be taken any time of the year, and recent additions also include a low ropes course, a purpose-built tunnelling system and bungee trampolines. Figures for 2007–08 show that over 13,000 girls used the climbing facilities there, and abseiling and the crate challenge were popular too.

Ever heard of Netherurd?

Each weekend throughout the year, Leaders and Guides make their way to the stunning surroundings of Netherurd House. This country mansion, set in 30 acres in the Scottish Border hills of Peeblesshire, has been the Training Centre for Girlguiding Scotland since 1945 when Major E. G. Thomson leased it to the Association for seven years. When the lease ran out the major generously donated the estate to the cause. The sparsely furnished but solidly built stone house, in Georgian style, was perfect for those attending the early courses, with plenty of accommodation for both trainees and staff, and large spacious reception rooms which were used as training rooms.

Over time, many refurbishments have taken place and it now boasts conference facilities, meeting rooms, a cosy library and even a small bar. Interior features have been preserved, however, and many a Leader has sought refuge from the biting Scottish weather by the open log fires in the original Adam fireplaces!

The latest addition to the facilities is the Garden House, which consists of three linked pavilions with accommodation for 60. Each wing has its own kitchen, dining room, lounge and laundry and is set in its own walled garden. There is also a high-dependency suite for Guides with special needs. Activities have also changed since 1945, with kayaking, raft-building, pioneering and abseiling among those on offer.

A hand of friendship

In the early 1990s, Netherurd became a weekend retreat for some of the most underprivileged families from nearby Edinburgh. Chief Commissioner Jean-Claire Schaw-Miller felt that the house and its grounds offered the perfect opportunity for single mothers and families to enjoy a much-needed break.

Edinburgh Division Commissioner Liz Pitcairn was asked to lead the project, in which seven mothers and fourteen children were referred by community support groups.

The first weekend was a great success. The mothers enjoyed relaxation classes, health and beauty sessions, and a shopping trip in Peebles, while their children got a taste of country life and had a wonderful time climbing trees, paddling in the burn and toasting marshmallows. The women and children bonded well and enjoyed a reunion three months later. One mother from the group went on to get various guiding qualifications, and is still in guiding today.

In 1992 the project expanded, with the Dundee Holiday Project, which ran until 2007.

Life at Lorne

For Guides all over Northern Ireland, Lorne House, which was bought by the Ulster Guides in 1946, holds special memories. The baronial-style building, set in 21 acres of Ulster countryside, takes its name from the family home of the Campbell Clan and was built by Henry Campbell in 1875.

Until 1946, Guiders from Northern Ireland took part in training weeks at Foxlease or Waddow, or in the training camps run by instructors travelling from mainland UK, in order to achieve their Camp Training Certificates and Diplomas.

With the increasing number of Guides the need for a permanent training centre became clear in the 1930s. However, the onset of the Second World War meant that developments were put on hold, until 1943, when a training camp at Knocktarna near Coleraine, so impressed Major Lyle that he offered his home and gardens for a nominal rent during his absence in England.

Knocktarna House opened as a training centre in 1944 but, at the same time, an appeal was launched to raise funds for a permanent centre. The Duchess of Abercorn challenged each member to raise £1, and by 1946 there was £6,107 in the fund. Along with a grant from the Ministry of Education, there was enough to purchase Lorne House, then an overgrown estate in County Down.

As the house had been uninhabited for some time, a great deal of work had to be done, and the house opened to Guides in 1947.

Journalist Joanne Mace remembers her time at Lorne with great affection:

I was lucky enough to go to guide camp at Lorne both as a Guide and as a Young Leader. We always slept in large tents in the fantastic grounds, except for one occasion when the unrelenting rain caused a mass movement indoors to take over the corridors and every available inch of space.

The brilliant timetabled events included archery, woodcraft and cookery, when we made buns in an oven which we'd made from a large tin can. I also remember being tasked with building a shelter from nothing but natural materials.

It was great to meet guides from all over Northern Ireland, and to have fun in an environment which was a vanity-free zone. We were able to escape from television and technology, sitting around campfires singing songs in the round before heading back to our tents, where we'd whisper in the dark until we feel asleep.

FAR LEFT: Our base in Northern Ireland

RIGHT TOP AND BOTTOM: Brownies have fun at Lorne

A Welsh retreat

Visitors to Broneirion, which nestles in the side of a steep, wooded valley overlooking the River Severn and the village of Llandinam, must first cross a bridge where a statue of the original owner, David Davies, surveys all who pass.

In 1946 Lady Eldrydd Davies offered the use of the house as a training centre for Welsh Guides. The cost of setting it up proved daunting, but an appeal soon saw gifts of furniture and soft furnishings pouring in. Each Welsh county adopted a room which, over the years, they have refurbished and cared for, and a committee was formed to run the centre.

In 1968, the World Chief Guide was present to launch the 'Friends of Broneirion', which is still well supported and instrumental in providing funds for refurbishment and development. It was not until 1992, however, that the house was purchased by Girlguiding Cymru as a Training and Activity Centre. An appeal for funds to do so raised enough to buy the house, set up a small endowment fund to take care of repairs and renovations, and buy a much-needed campsite close to the property which was renamed Cae Gwenllian, in honour of former Chief Commissioner the Hon. Gwenllian Phillips.

A Duke's legacy

Broneirion is set in four and a half acres of azaleas, rhododendrons and daffodils, and is also the site of the first Wellingtonia trees to be planted in Wales. These trees, similar to the Californian Redwood, were discovered by plant hunter William Lobb 1854 and became popular with Victorians as specimen plants.

In Britain, the tree was named *Wellingtonia gigantea*, after the recently deceased Duke of Wellington, but the Americans wanted to call it Washingtonia, after their first president. Years of debate led to the official name becoming *Sequoiadendron giganteum*, although the beautiful trees at Broneirion, which now tower over the house, are still known to visitors as Wellingtonias.

Broneirion was officially reopened on 29 June 1993 by the Hon. Betty Clay, daughter of Lord and Lady Baden-Powell. Two years later the cottage at the gate of the estate, Broneirion Lodge, was also purchased.

It is as it has always been, a story of enterprise; its results are great. Let us look back and give thanks and look forward and take courage.
Miss Heather Kay on Broneirion

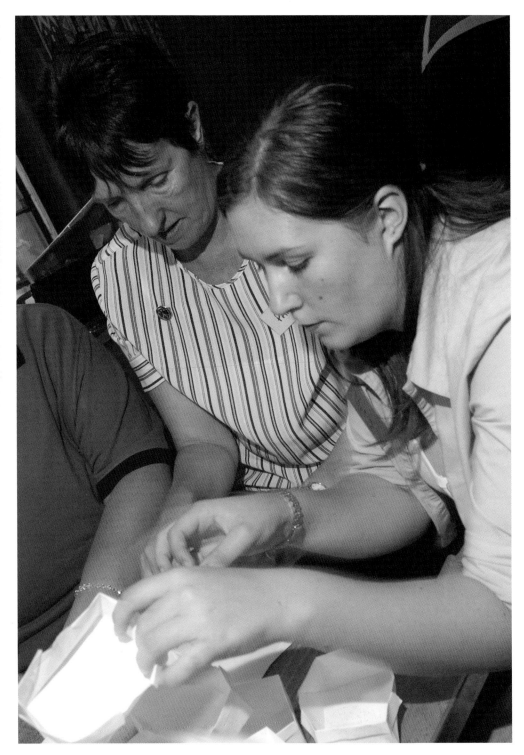

A gift from Norfolk broads

Former rectory Hautbois was bequeathed to the Girl Guides in 1984, by two sisters who had devoted themselves to guiding all their lives. Beth and Philippa Patteson had lived in the beautiful riverside house, near the Norfolk Broads, from birth. At nine, an illness left Philippa partially sighted, and when she joined the Guides Beth was given dispensation to join early to help her older sister.

As adults the sisters helped run the local Brownies and Guides and allowed them to meet in the schoolroom in the grounds, as well as using the 28 acres of land for outdoor activities. At the top of the house, there is a small window which opens on to the roof top. Legend has it that Beth would often climb out and use semaphore flags to signal to the Guides down below. The room was also utilised as a makeshift 'hospital' for the First Aid training, at which Philippa excelled.

The two ladies, who never married, were often visited by Olave Baden-Powell at the house and Beth eventually rose to the rank of County Commissioner.

Although the sisters have passed on, it is said that their spirits can often be seen walking on the terrace at night – no doubt keeping an eye on the Guides visiting the estate!

LEFT: In the grounds of Hautbois

LEFT: Hautbois

RIGHT: Learning survival skills at Hautbois

Peak of fitness

Nestling in nine acres in the Peak District National Park, Glenbrook Outdoor Activities Centre is located between the villages of Hope and Hathersage. It offers holidays for the units, Leader weekends and training courses predominantly of hillwalking. The main house sleeps 30, while the distinctive 'tent-shaped' Derwent house and two flats hold 49 more. Girls can play volleyball and boules, go pony trekking, orienteering, 'weaselling' (squeezing beneath rocks) and stream-dipping, or climb a bouldering wall for a fun-packed break.

On the beach

Ynysgain, managed by Girlguiding Cymru, is set in farmland on the outskirts of Snowdonia National Park, and is just five minutes' walk from a beautiful beach. Here visitors to the three campsites can share the shores with seals and sea birds, in between walking, climbing and watersports.

The challenges are much more fun and exciting than they were when I was a Guide. They seem to get involved in more outdoor things now, from a younger age. Our Guides and some Young Leaders went to Pax Wood recently and had a pamper weekend! The Guides and Young Leaders stayed overnight and did tasks to do with food and health, and the next morning someone came and made their faces up and showed them how to make home-made moisturising creams and beauty products. They are very health conscious in the Guides today.

Ann Ferguson, Leader and a Guide in the 1970s

Fashionistas

The Brownies' and Guides' most radical makeover took place in the 1990s. Designer Jeff Banks, then presenter of *The Clothes Show*, took into account the 10,000 questionnaires from members detailing what they wanted to wear. Jeff did away with the dreaded A-line skirt and took a more practical approach, designing a mix-and-match range that included culottes, polo shirts, sweatshirts, a

blouse and jogging bottoms. The hat was replaced with an optional baseball cap and the badges were worn on a navy sash across their uniform.

Before finalising his designs, he showed them to the Association's President, HRH Princess Margaret, who vetoed formal navy blue uniforms, telling him 'I don't want them to look like policewomen'.

The Princess also got her own specially designed outfit, which included a navy blue skirt, double-breasted jacket and plain white blouse, all of wool gabardine. The unveiling of the collection, at a fashion show in Westminster, was later shown on *The Clothes Show*. The designer, who gave his time free, explained: 'Hopefully, I have produced a range that will mean activities should be more pleasurable for the Guides and not an endurance test. Culottes, for instance, are much more practical than a skirt for scrambling up Snowdon!'

FAR LEFT TOP AND ABOVE: Jeff Banks's original sketches, which differed significantly from the finished designs

FAR LEFT: 1990 Brownie uniform

LEFT: Members from all the sections in uniform, 2008

Ally Capellino

BELOW: Designer Ally Capellino

LEFT: A Rainbow, a Brownie and a Guide in uniform, 2008

RIGHT: Senior Section members in their hoodies, 2008

As the 21st century dawned, the look was in for another revamp, courtesy of top designer Ally Capellino, whose clients include Kate Moss and Sadie Frost. She added a new T-shirt, body-warmer, rugby shirt and sweatshirt for Guides, to be worn with jeans, leggings or shorts. The brown and yellow Brownies range included hooded jackets, boot-cut leggings, a gilet, T-shirts and skorts (shorts with a flat front like a skirt) to be worn with a brown sash for badges.

In 2004 Capellino swapped the sleeveless tabards of the Rainbows for a new uniform of a red hooded jacket, jogging pants, cycle shorts and a red and blue polo shirt. The current Senior Section uniform includes a two-tone rugby shirt, blouse, hooded top and polo shirt.

A competition held in 2007 to design the 'hoodie' was won by four Senior Section members who then travelled to India to see their artistic creation become a reality. Ever mindful of the ethical aspects of textile production, the girls did an audit of the working conditions in the factory too, thus combining a flair for design with concern for the welfare of others.

The first Guide fashions

The unofficial costume of the girls at the 1909 Crystal Palace Rally, which was adapted from their brothers' Scout uniform, was replaced by an official look soon after the founding of the movement.

In his *Scheme for Girl Guides*, Lord Baden-Powell suggested a dark blue uniform with a pale blue tie and a red biretta, alternating with a straw hat for the summer months. The girls, who instantly took against the biretta, showed typical guiding initiative by dyeing the large Scout hats navy blue. This led to the introduction in 1911 of a similar hat in blue with a hat ribbon bearing the letters BPGG, for Baden-Powell Girl Guides (although some believed that the BP stood for 'Be Prepared'!).

The hemline of the A-line serge or flannel skirt was raised to mid-calf and was worn with sturdy black buttoned boots and stockings of wool or cashmere. The tie, knotted at the neck, was also knotted at the bottom if a good deed was still to be done. Brown leather gauntlet gloves, leather belts, capes, lanyards, haversacks and even stretcher slings were issued as part of the uniform, although the last two were phased out in the early 1920s.

The post-war period saw the biggest change in the uniform since its inception. In 1946 the new brighter blue shirt, to be worn inside a navy skirt, was introduced – the colour soon became known as 'Guide Blue'. The shirt and skirt were worn with brown shoes and stockings and a beret with a trefoil badge.

In the mid-1960s, the beret was replaced by a navy blue, air hostess-style cap and the blouse by an open-necked rayon design with pockets at the bottom instead of at the breast. Several new tie styles were tried out until in 1969 the tie became a crossover. Lanyards and shoulder knots were out and man-made fabrics were in, with polyester, rayon and worsted taking the place of flannel.

As mini-skirts were the must-have fashion of the day, the late '60s also saw hemlines creeping way above the knees.

The uniform of the 1960s remained largely unchanged until Jeff Banks's radical redesign in 1990.

Marjorie Seal started as a Leader in Kent in the early 1960s. She remembers:

We had screens for each Patrol and one of the diagrams pinned on it was how to fold a tie. The ties were triangular then, so that they could be used as a sling, or a bandage, in an emergency. We started the meeting with a roll-call and then three girls would present the colours – put the flag up. Then we would have company inspection, when we would check they had a reef knot in their tie, that their shoes were clean, look at hands and nails and then the contents of their pockets. The uniforms had breast pockets and the girls would have to carry paper and a pen or pencil, a coin in case they had to make a phone call, a piece of string and a safety pin.

Brownies

As Rosebuds, the younger branch of the Guide movement started with an unofficial uniform of a dark blue jumper and skirt, switching to an optional brown dress with white collar and the addition of a rush hat trimmed with brown with the name change in 1915.

In 1917 the brown tunic dress was introduced, with an alternative knitted cap, a brown belt and a tie. An optional gold tie and a cloth cap to replace the knitted one arrived in the 1930s, and was in turn replaced with the familiar wool beret in the 1950s.

In 1967 a cotton dress with pockets in the skirt was introduced and the new Promise badge, featuring a Brownie pixie inside a trefoil, was worn on the new yellow tie. The popular bobble hat officially came into being in 1973. The most radical change for Brownies came when trousers were permitted for the first time in 1977.

Senior Section

The first Cadets wore either their old Guide uniform or their school uniform with a white hat band, hat badge and triangular tie to distinguish them from Guides. Rangers wore a red hat badge and the Sea Rangers' uniform consisted of a navy blue jumper and skirt with a navy blue hat and black tie.

During the Second World War, Land Rangers switched to a grey jersey with a navy blue tie and a blue beret with a red hat badge. The merging of the Land, Sea, Air and Cadet Rangers in 1967 meant an altogether new look, with an aquamarine blouse, navy skirt and navy hat, and, a few years on, a navy pinafore dress was offered as an alternative. Young Leaders were allowed to wear the uniform from 1973.

LEFT: Brownie uniform in 1950

RIGHT: The new mini-skirts were in style by the time this 1973 annual was published

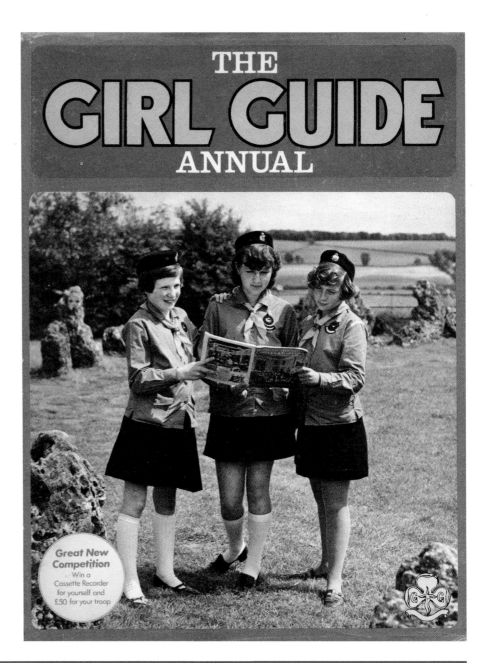

THE GIRL GUIDE ANNUAL

Great New Competition
Win a Cassette Recorder for yourself and £50 for your troop

Growing Up

Today girls can be involved in guiding from the age of five (four in Northern Ireland), and progress from Rainbows through Brownies, Guides, the Senior Section and the Trefoil Guild – there is no upper age limit, with some ex-Guides still active in their 90s.

Rainbows

Rainbows are the youngest, not just in terms of members' age but also the age of the section itself. In fact, in 2008 it celebrated its 21st birthday with a series of parties and events. Rainbows currently number around 80,000, with 6,500 units in the UK, and one in seven six-year-olds is a member.

Each step in the movement marks a stage in the growth of the child. Rainbows start developing and thinking for themselves, in a safe girl-only environment. The children take part in activities in four 'Jigsaw' areas, encouraging them to Look, Learn, Laugh and Love, and have to make a simple Promise: 'I promise that I will do my best to love my

God and to be kind and helpful'. The girls can carry on the fun at home with the activities and games designed specially for them on the Rainbow website. While they are too young to camp, the girls can take part in an overnight event, such as a sleepover, with their Leaders.

Although the section was not officially set up until 1987, the origins may lie in the Bunny Scheme for young girls in Northern Ireland in the 1950s. The scheme caught the attention of the Trefoil Guild, who lent their support, and in 1978 the Guild decided to adopt the Bunnies as their special project during the International Year of the Child.

By 1983 there were 3,000 Bunnies in Northern Ireland. Two years later it was agreed that Bunnies could become part of the Guide movement if they and their Leaders made the Promise. In approving the move, the Executive Committee had tacitly agreed to similar groups starting up in the UK, and set about producing a programme for younger girls.

A name change for the section was first on the agenda, although Ulster felt that it would be wrong to change from Bunnies after 35 years; and Bunnies started at the age of four, while the

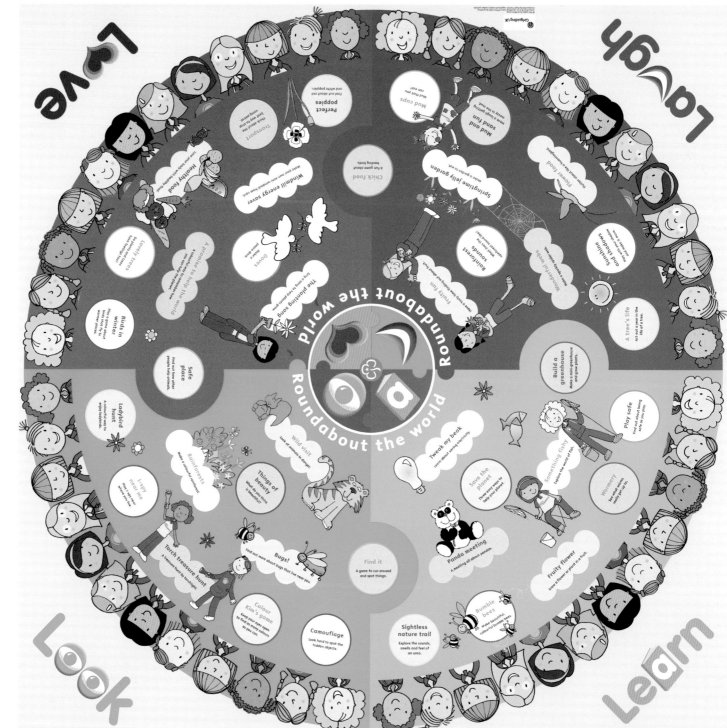

RIGHT: The Rainbow Roundabout

TOP: The first Rainbow Promise badge, worn on the tunic

BOTTOM: The Rainbow Roundabout badge

Association's recommendation was a minimum age of six. However, the differences were soon ironed out and the name Rainbow was agreed.

In June 1987 guidelines for Rainbows were published and the following spring a starter pack and the colourful tabards of red, blue, green and yellow went on sale. Later in 1988 units were able to register under the same group name as Brownies and Guides. In 1991 the starting age was dropped to the girl's fifth birthday, except in Ulster where it remains the start date of her primary education. Since the early days both the uniform and the girls' programme have been reviewed and changed from time to time to ensure that they are always exciting and modern.

When a Rainbow is about six months away from turning seven, she completes a 'Pot of Gold' challenge and plans a party. Around her seventh birthday, she has a 'Pot of Gold' party and her fellow Rainbows say goodbye. She is ready to become a Brownie.

RIGHT: The 1st
Hadham Rosebud
Pack in 1914

ABOVE: Rosebud Promise
badge 1914–1915

Brownies (and Rosebuds)

With the step up to Brownies, the horizon expands once again. New and exciting activities make up the Brownie adventure, and girls can go camping for the first time – an important step on their road to independence. They also gain interest badges and develop great understanding in the three adventure areas of You, the Community and the World.

The millions of Brownies around the world owe a debt to younger sisters who were not content to sit by while the older girls had all the fun. In the early years, the popularity of the Guide movement soon rubbed off on the Guides' younger siblings and, in many cases, it was impossible for some of the older ones to come to meetings without bringing their smaller charges. As meetings took place, they were often watched by a ring of eager faces for whom the long wait until their 11th birthday must have seemed interminable.

In 1914 the younger children began to be organised into groups for activities and training, so it was decided that a new section should be set up for them: they were named Rosebuds, to reflect how these 'buds' would blossom into roses. These were the first 'Brownies', though they were not yet named as such.

The Rosebuds wore dark blue uniforms and were taught their own salute, using two fingers instead of the three the Guides used. The Association proceeded cautiously at first, introducing a minimum age of eight and a list of the many challenges that Rosebuds could NOT do. 'A Rosebud may not wear Girl Guide uniform hat. Neither may she wear any Girl Guide badges,' stated Agnes Baden-Powell. She did, however, design a badge for them, and a special password was devised, 'Dubesor a uoyera?' (which is 'Are you a Rosebud?' backwards), to which the reply was 'Duba Mai' (i.e., 'I am a Bud').

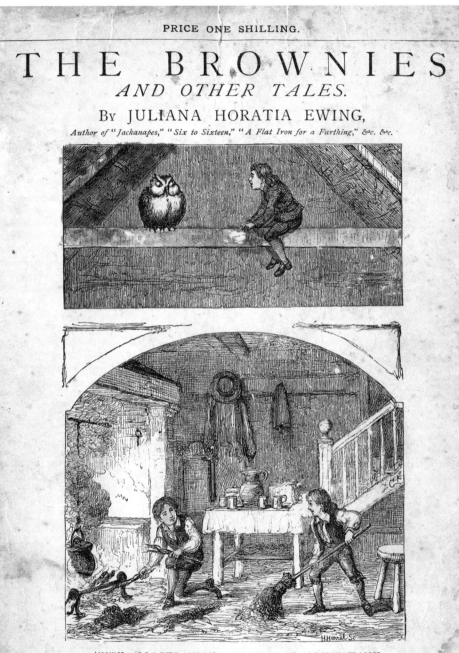

PRICE ONE SHILLING.

THE BROWNIES
AND OTHER TALES.

By JULIANA HORATIA EWING,

Author of "Jackanapes," "Six to Sixteen," "A Flat Iron for a Farthing," &c. &c.

WITH ILLUSTRATIONS BY GEORGE CRUIKSHANK.

London:
GEORGE BELL AND SONS, YORK STREET, COVENT GARDEN.

A Rosebud had to be proficient in certain skills: she had to know how the Union Flag is made up, and how to fly it, how to tie a series of knots and to be able to do six bending exercises specified in the 1912 *Guiding Handbook*. Girls were encouraged to breathe through the nose and to pray while doing exercises for the upper body, liver, back, stomach, lower body and legs.

The young girls were delighted with the new section but were not impressed by the name and in 1915 asked that it be changed. Suggestions mooted included Kittens, Diddies, Juniors, Mice and Rats, but the most popular was 'Brownies', suggested by Robert Baden-Powell and inspired by a book by Juliana Ewing, *The Brownies and Other Tales*, which he adapted. In fact, the children in the original story were both boys, called Tommy and Johnnie Trout, and it was not until 1918 that Baden-Powell changed Johnnie to Betty for the second *Guiding Handbook, Girl Guiding.* As well as the change to the section title, patrols were named after British trees,

Brownie Tests in 1915

Entrance Test

- Know how to wash up the tea things.
- Clean and fill salt cellar or hem handkerchief or duster.
- Plait her own hair.
- Tie her own tie.

Badge: round badge with an acorn

Second Class Test

- Know how the Union Flag is composed and what it means.
- Make her own necktie or cap.
- Do up a parcel neatly.
- Lay a table for dinner for four.
- Darn stockings.
- Bind up a cut finger or knee.
- Know and perform three of the physical exercises given in the *Guiding Handbook*.

Badge: the Acorn badge with leaves

First Class Test

- Clean knives, spoons, forks.
- Clean boots, and know how to dry them when wet.
- Make doll's clothes (clothes may be ready cut out) or make a Brownie overall.
- Fold clothes for mangling.
- Knit a pair of socks or wristlets.
- Know how to apply triangular bandage.
- Understand and carry out six physical exercises.
- Make a milk pudding.
- Carry a message of 12 words in her head and deliver it correctly.

FAR LEFT:
The Brownies and Other Tales, published in the 1870s

TOP LEFT: Athlete badge and First Aider badge, 1917

TOP RIGHT: The Acorn badge for the Second Class Test, 1915

the motto of 'Lend a Hand' was introduced and a brown uniform began to replace the blue. The Company Leader soon became Brown Owl, after the Wise Brown Owl in Mrs Ewing's stories, and a metal badge, bearing the image of an acorn, was designed.

In 1917 proficiency badges were introduced and divided into four groups – Character and Intelligence, Skill and Handicraft, Service for Others, and Physical Health – with different-coloured badges. 'Patrols' became 'Sixes' and the names changed from trees to fairy folk, such as Gnomes, Elves and Imps. The reason given for this was that a tree was 'a great slow-growing, quiet and passive sort of beast, whereas a Brownie is just about the opposite of this'.

The publication of Robert Baden-Powell's *Girl Guiding: A Handbook for Guidelets, Guides, Senior Guides and Guiders* in 1918 meant a more organised Brownie programme, and in 1920 the first *Brownie Handbook* finally appeared.

The Brownie Law, which was introduced in 1920, read:

1. The Brownie gives in to the older folk
2. The Brownie does not give in to herself.

By now girls over nine were joining in camps with the company of Guides to which they were attached, and sleeping in tents with Guides so they would not get frightened at night. By 1921 there were 59,352 Brownies in the UK. This figure rose to 161,765 by 1945.

Throughout their history Brownies have proved as hardy and helpful as their older counterparts. During the 1920s and 1930s they sent Christmas gifts to children in the far-flung corners of the British Empire, collected clothes for the miners hit by the General Strike of 1926 and in the Great Depression knitted squares for quilts, sewed tablecloths and collected shells in the Guide Trails for Service. Brownies also visited almshouses and donated white sticks for the blind as well as inviting poor city children down to the country for a week's holiday. Their helpful skills were reflected in a new rash of badges – Jester in 1921, Thrift in 1924, Needlework

in 1927, Book Lover, Musician, Writer and Toymaker in 1932 and Knitter in 1935.

During the Second World War their services proved useful once again, and at the end of the war Brownie Holidays were resumed, though parents had to secure emergency ration cards for participating girls. The cost of a child travelling 40 miles for a holiday was between 15 and 22 shillings, a considerable amount to find in those austere days.

Despite their own hardships the Brownies still remembered those less fortunate. They continued to send equipment and gifts to their counterparts in the displaced persons camps and as late as 1954 Guides and Brownies raised enough money to invite two Latvian girls from one camp for a holiday. One keen Brownie single-handedly organised a fête and raised £1 to help.

At the same time, Brownies elsewhere were helping the UK, sending food parcels from around the world and, in 1951, the Brownie Exhibition at Headquarters was given a huge

boost by the arrival of 40 food parcels from Australia. In 1948, the national Guide Finance Scheme came into effect, with Brownies paying a halfpenny a week (one shilling and sixpence a year) to Guide Headquarters. (Guides and Rangers paid a penny a week or three shillings a year.) The fee stayed the same for 15 years, when it was raised to a penny a week or three shillings a year, while the Guides paid four shillings and sixpence a year.

The Brownie branch continued to thrive throughout the 1950s, providing a considerable presence at the 13th World Conference and taking part in the Queen's Coronation celebrations. The theme of global awareness became an integral part of the programme, with the Brownie World badge introduced in 1955. Indeed, in 1957 Brownies continued the theme, by pledging to do six World Good Turns with the theme 'Houses of Today and Tomorrow'.

The 1960s was a boom period for the younger section. In 1963, for example, one in eight girls between seven and eleven was a Brownie and by 1965 there were 313,382 members. Activities were changing too. For instance, as so few homes had open fires, washing and ironing a Brownie tie was given as an alternative First Class clause to laying and lighting a fire. In 1963 the change in methods was indicated by an article in the *Guider* on the pros and cons of using modern short cuts in test work, such as sticky

tape (instead of string), plasters (instead of bandages) and cake mix. The writer rejected the newfangled short cuts as expensive and less of a challenge for the Brownie. And Brownies do love a challenge and always rise to the occasion. As the Girl Guides celebrated their 75th anniversary in 1985 the Brownies refused to be left out of the party. They were given a month-long task by the Tea Council to 'turn a cup of tea into a meal for a hungry child'. Girls up and down the country sold tea at 10p a cup – the amount needed to buy a meal for a child in the Third World – and raised a staggering £179,000 for Save the Children. The girls who proved the most enterprising, the 77th Blackburn Brownie Pack, were rewarded with tea at the Savoy Hotel with HRH Princess Anne.

Today one in four of all eight-year-old girls in the UK is a Brownie. Just like their older sisters, Brownies have evolved over time and their uniform and activities have changed accordingly. Their meetings are full of challenges, games and activities, usually ones that the girls have suggested themselves. The Brownie website builds on these and offers the girls the chance to have fun at home too.

Their badges include Science Investigator, Computer, Designer and Dancer, and older Brownies take part in a programme called *Brownies Go for It!* which allows for more independence, develops leadership skills and encourages them to find out more about the Guides before moving up.

TOP: Brownie badges

Badge of Honour

Enthusiastic girls were earning badges even before the Guide movement began, albeit by subterfuge. In February 1909, for example, a group of six pupils fired by the start of the Boy Scout Movement got together at Lingholt School, Hindhead, and called themselves 'Night-Hawks'. With the encouragement of their headmistress, they were allowed to 'Scout' for half an hour a day and, when a second Patrol calling themselves 'Wildcats' was formed, they waged a friendly war each night. The pupil wrote:

BOTH PAGES:
Various badges from the 1930s on

This thrilling life lasted for over a year, during which we gained many badges. But alas, Boy Scout headquarters finally discovered that we were girls, and demanded the return of our badges.

(We had obtained them by the device of giving our initials only, not our Christian names, when applying!)

Luckily, change was on the horizon, and a year later the girls were registered as 1st Hindhead troop and could concentrate on earning their badges legitimately. As befitted the times, some of the first Guide badges were rather more genteel than the Scout badges of the day, including Florist, Clerk, Cook and Matron. However, as is evident from the lists of badges below, the badges became more adventurous as time went on.

First Interest badges

Artist
Clerk
Cook
Cyclist
Electrician
Farmer (became Dairymaid in 1912 and Landworker in 1917)
First Aid (became Ambulance in 1914; later reverted to First Aid)
Florist (renamed Gardener in 1916)
Gymnast
Hospital Nurse (became Sick Nurse in 1912)
Matron (renamed Housekeeper in 1916)
Musician
Nurse (became Child Nurse 1912)
Pioneer

Sailor (became Boatswain in 1912)
Signaller
Tailor (later became Needlewoman)
Telegraphist

1911

Horsemanship (renamed Horsewoman in 1914)
Pathfinder

1912

Fire Brigade
Flyer (renamed Air Mechanic in 1917)
Laundress
Rifle Shot

1914

Photographer

During the First World War the emphasis on practical skills was heightened, and with so many men and boys away at war, or employed in the war effort, the girls learnt skills that were traditionally considered male preserves. The introduction of such badges as Carpenter, Cobbler, Poultry Farmer and Handywoman reflected the need for everyone to muck in.

1916
Astronomer
Carpenter
Cobbler
Entertainer
Bee Farmer
Basket Weaver
Friend to animals
Geologist
Handywoman
Knitter
Milliner
Surveyor

1917
Dairymaid (new design)
Thrift
Poultry Farmer
Dancer
Domestic Service
Embroideress (became Lacemaker in 1919)

1919
Athlete
Sportswoman
Toymaker

1920
Authoress
Health

By the 1950s, one or two badges had disappeared, including the now irrelevant Domestic Service. Additional badges included Rabbit Keeper, Interpreter to the Deaf (later renamed Friend to the Deaf) and Emergency Helper. For their Homemaker badge, Guides were expected to lay and light a fire in a grate, make beds and make a jam or a pickle, while the Commonwealth badge had them learning about a UK dependent territory and keeping a scrapbook about it.

Some badges from 1957
Fire Brigade
Interpreter
Interpreter to the Deaf
Emergency Helper
Map Reader
Rabbit Keeper
Thrift
Hostess
Cook
Homemaker

TOP LEFT:
1st Charlsbury Girl Guides with evacuees from Shoreditch practise signalling, 1940

Go for It!

Over the 100 years since the foundation of the movement, the interests, hobbies and perceptions of the Guides have changed dramatically, and so too have the badges. From Confectioner to Circus skills and from Science to Survival skills, there's something for everyone. Here are some of the exciting challenges the Guides can take on today, with some comments from the Guides themselves. Oddly enough, it seems the badges that revolve around sweets and chocolate are the most popular!

Outdoor pursuits

Those who enjoy the outdoors have a wonderful time gaining this badge. Girls choose at least two activities from a list of 13, including abseiling, rafting, sailing and skiing, and as well as participating must discuss suitable clothing, learn safety regulations and find out about the professional qualifications connected to these activities.

I have tried archery, go-karting and gone on residential and day trips. I love doing the art and craft and I've learnt things relevant to some Go for Its!, like sewing. My favourite night was our enrolment night – we had a beauty pamper night!
Rosie, 3rd Burton Latimer Guides

Chocolate badge

Girls are asked to find out the history of chocolate and how it came into the UK, to learn about fair trade, design a chocolate wrapper and make up a game involving chocolate. Then comes the best bit – she must provide a variety of chocolate products for tasting with her Patrol and make a selection of sweets. Yummy!

I loved making things with chocolate and learning about the history of chocolate and fair trade.
Ellie, 80th Newcastle-upon-Tyne (Holy Cross) Guides

Camper

Camper incorporates many of the traditional skills associated with guiding. The Guide must help to pitch a tent, spend two nights under canvas, light a fire and prepare, cook, serve and clear away a meal. She must also learn how to look after bedding and do simple first aid.

I love going on the camps and I've learnt to light fires and cook food.
Charlotte, 2nd Morpeth Guides

ABOVE:
Modern badges

Party planner

For the budding events organiser, this is both fun and good training. First she must choose an occasion to celebrate – there will be plenty of these badges handed out over the Centenary Year! Then she must organise the event, either by herself or with her group, and carry out three actions herself, such as inviting a special guest, producing a menu and cooking a dish. Then it's party time!

Circus skills

The girls can really clown about to gain this badge! The Guide must take part in a circus workshop and then learn three more skills, for example, juggling, diabolo, unicycling or plate spinning.

Science

This may be a badge for the Marie Curies of the future but it still involves sweets! Three of the eight tasks suggested, of which the Guide must achieve four, involve making, eating or finding out about confectionery. Alternatively, Guides can study plants and animals, design a measuring device or find out about the manufacture of clothes.

Film lover

This is a great badge for the cinema buff. Participants watch five films chosen from 11 different categories, such as romance, Western, comedy or mystery, and then write a review of the films. The Guide must also discuss a favourite actor or director and explain the classification system. As a Go for It! challenge she can even take it further and make a film of her own with her Patrol.

My favourite activity was making a video for our Go for It! Lights, camera, action!
Polly, 12th Ramsgate West

World issues

Teaching the girls about the lives of others and encouraging them to help is a core objective of the movement, and this badge brings the issues to life. Tasks include carrying a heavy bucket of water to replicate the daily toil of many women, keeping a diary of journeys and making a birthday card using recycled paper.

Through the ages

While many of the badges today could not have been imagined in 1910, most have an equivalent from the early days. For example, the Signaller and Telegraphist badges, introduced before the First World War, have strong similarities with the modern Communicator.

Hostess, introduced in 1957, bears a striking resemblance to Party Planner; the 1916 Entertainer badge has become Performing arts; and Health from 1920 changed to Fitness in 1983 and is now Healthy lifestyles.

Many badges, such as First Aid, Cook and Camper have kept the same name while the programmes have evolved to move with the times.

All Grown Up

LEFT: Senior Section Promise badge

RIGHT: Leader Promise badge

ABOVE: Senior Section girls on a camping weekend in 2006

The Senior Section, which caters for 14–25 year-olds, has seen the most changes in structure and composition of any branch of the movement. It is currently comprised of Rangers, Young Leaders, Junior Council members, student groups and Duke of Edinburgh Award participants, and is designed to be flexible, fun and challenging, especially at a time when older girls may be preparing to leave home for the first time.

The idea that girls over 16 would enjoy activities similar to those enjoyed by Guides first emerged in 1916. The original members and some who had joined since were getting too

old for their companies, while other older girls, particularly those over 16 who had been working in munitions factories in the First World War, were keen to join for the first time. Older groups began to spring up and at the same time the first Cadet Companies, aimed at training girls to become Guide Leaders, were started in girls' schools.

In 1917 Robert Baden-Powell asked an Executive Committee member called Rose Kerr to take on the Senior Guides, as they had come to be known. In organising the older Guides she was careful to take their different circumstances into account. In 1918 she wrote in the *Girl Guides' Gazette*:

Any Guide over 16 is eligible for promotion to Senior Guides. It must be remembered that nearly all Senior Guides will have been working hard during the day and will want recreation in the evening. They should not therefore be encouraged to do badge work in the evenings; their time should be spent principally in games, singing, country dancing and other occupations affording a complete change from their day-time employments.

Among Rose Kerr's first tasks was to find a new name: suggestions included Pioneers, Rovers, Citizen Guides, Pilots, Torchbearers, Eagerhearts and Guides-women! On the train back to London from the Swanwick Conference in 1920, Mrs Kerr asked the Chief Scout for help. He said:

I always think it's a good thing to take a vague name, with which people have not got any very definite association. Then one can put one's own meaning into it and create a tradition. When we were discussing names for the Senior Scouts 'Rover' and 'Ranger' were both suggested. We decided on 'Rover'. Why should you not take 'Ranger' for the Senior Guides?

The name was duly approved in July 1920 at the Oxford Conference, and the same year a branch of seafaring seniors sprang up, named Sea Guides. The three Senior groups were brought together in 1927, and became known as Rangers, Sea Rangers and Cadet Rangers.

A name explained

Extract from the Chief Guide's letter to the *Girl Guides' Gazette*, June 1920.

Here is the suggested new name: 'Ranger'. If you look it up in the dictionary you will find it means quite a number of things. 'To range' is 'to set a proper order'; 'to roam', and this might well mean that you are going to tread ground as a Senior Guide that as a Guide you have not yet passed.

'Distance of Vision, and extent of discourse or roaming power' again shows that as a senior member of the community you are expected to look farther afield for good and work that you can do for the community.

A Ranger is 'one who guards a large tract of forest or land', thus it comes to mean one who has a wide outlook, and sense of responsible protective duties, appropriate to a Senior Guide.

Another definition is 'to sail along in a parallel direction', and so we can feel that the Ranger Guides are complementary to the Rover Scouts.

And so we hope that this new title will have the approval of all.

RIGHT: Rangers take part in a salvage drive mass semaphore in July 1943

FAR RIGHT: Rangers helping out the ATS in 1943

But Rangers were not the only ones interested in life on the open sea – Guides soon got in on the act. It was decreed in 1932 that girls between 14 and 16 could join a Sea Guide Patrol and be attached to a ship's company, and would wear a tally band on their hats to distinguish them from Sea Rangers. Formal training for Sea Rangers began on HMS *Implacable* and HMS *Foudroyant* at Portsmouth in 1937, and units adopted the names of real navy vessels and kept in touch with the crews in the coming war years. When HMS *Royal Oak* went down, for example, one of her officers wrote to SRS *Royal Oak*: 'We have sunk, but you must carry on our name for the present.'

The Second World War saw the older girls becoming increasingly useful but, with a shortage of young men to work at essential jobs in factories, many of them were drafted into full-time work. More capable hands were needed for the vital voluntary work and, as a result, the Executive Committee felt it was time to drop the age limit from 16 to 14, where it remains today.

The Sea Rangers were now joined by the Air Rangers, whose units were known as Flights and who undertook some

BELOW: Sea Rangers mending nets in 1928

training with the RAF. The year after the Second World War ended was a momentous one in the Rangers' history. Not only did Princess Margaret become a Sea Ranger, and join her sister Princess Elizabeth in the first course on training ship MTB 630, but there was a huge turnout at the All England Ranger Rally in London. The future Queen took the salute at the march past while Princesses Mary and Margaret were guests of honour at the pageant, held in the Albert Hall. The rally was repeated four years later, when 8,000 Rangers met at White City stadium and saluted Princess Margaret before marching to the Albert Hall for an evening of singing, speeches and activity displays.

The mid-1960s saw an extensive review of all the branches within the Senior Branch facing a radical overhaul. The Rangers, Sea Rangers, Air Rangers and Cadets amalgamated to become the Ranger Guide Service Section, and a new aquamarine uniform was designed. The move was controversial among existing members, who liked their specialist units as they were, but the Executive Committee felt that more Guides would be encouraged to join the Ranger Guides if the programme were more flexible. It was decided that the units could put off registering if they were unhappy with the changes, but by 1969 some 80 per cent of the groups had re-registered and new membership was up by 5,000. The gamble had paid off.

The Senior Section continued to thrive through the 1970s, when shared activities with the Scouts led to a working party being set up to provide future provision for mixed packs. The Queen's Guide badge, which had originally been for Guides under the age of 17 and then for the under-16s, was revised in 1981 to be available solely for girls between 16 and 19. Candidates for this challenging award could not start before their 16th birthday and had to complete

BELOW: Senior Section Guides in 2008

RIGHT: Adult
volunteers

RIGHT: Adult
volunteers

Volunteers: essential and highly valued

It's incredibly rewarding to watch a shy and nervous girl grow more and more outgoing and confident at each unit meeting.

I've made some wonderful friends and met people from all over the world through guiding. It's fantastic!
What Leaders think of volunteering

a number of challenges in five different areas, including Service in Guiding and Community Action, by their 19th birthday. A silver brooch replaced the badge in 1983, and was to be presented with a certificate from the Queen. Princess Margaret presented the first 50 brooches at Kensington Palace in 1986.

The Look Wider scheme was launched in 1994, named after a favourite phrase of Lord Baden-Powell – 'Look Wide! And when you are looking wider, look wider still.' The programme encourages members to start something new, then progress it further and, finally, to try for a qualification in their chosen activity. It is also linked to a variety of recognised qualifications or awards, both within and outside guiding. To suit their age and sense of independence, the programme for the Senior Section members is available to them on a CD.

By the year 2000, Young Leaders came under the wing of the Senior Section. Today, there are over 20,000 Senior Section Guides in 1,200 units. As well as helping to run Brownie and Guide units and training as Leaders, their activities range from abseiling to taking part in youth forums on issues that affect girls and young women.

Guiding has always relied on the passion, skills and dedication of volunteers to enable 'girls and young women to develop their potential and to make a difference to the world'. Over the years, volunteers have worked, with training and support, in a variety of roles, such as Unit helpers, instructors, Unit Leaders and Commissioners. They have taken part in exciting activities with the girls, getting involved in outdoor challenges, learning new skills, participating in community action projects and sometimes even travelling overseas.

There are currently 100,000 adults giving their time freely to help change the lives of over half a million girls and young women – and their own!

I've met so many inspiring people through guiding. The Leaders and other volunteers who give their time to make guiding happen are all extraordinary people living ordinary lives. It's great how our Leaders can come from all walks of life – doctors, policewomen, chemical engineers, journalists. They're just some of the amazing people who give up their time.
Jasmine Rahman, Senior Section member

Trefoil Guild

The Trefoil Guild, formed in 1943, is a group of over 20,000 women and men who have been, and still are, in some way connected with Guiding and Scouting. As well as bringing together those with special interests, the Guild reflects the religious diversity of guiding, with its Communities Guild for members from different religious backgrounds.

Ten years before the formation of the Trefoil Guild, when the Quo Vadis Council met to discuss 'the Guide Movement for Older Girls', the idea of an organisation for those who wanted to maintain their links with the movement in adulthood was mooted.

When discussing a maximum age range for Rangers, the Council concluded:

ABOVE: Trefoil Promise badge

LEFT: Trefoil Guild members

There is, of course, no reason why they should not keep in touch with their old companies by coming back to them on special occasions. It is, however, felt that there is a need for some sort of organisation to bind together the older members of the Guide and Scout Movement who no longer have the time to give to practical Scouting and Guiding, but who want to keep the Scout and Guide spirit in their lives. It should be possible to link such people up with each other so that they may continue to receive inspiration and so that they may, where possible, meet together in groups and find out ways of performing service.

The idea of Old Guides was discussed and the name Guidons was suggested by Robert Baden-Powell, who described them as the fourth cylinder in the Guides' engine. Eventually, the Executive Committee and the Branch Commissioners agreed to form a Trefoil Guild, and details

were finally published in *The Guider*. In 1984, the idea was extended to include men who had been involved in Scouting.

The Hon. Betty Clay, daughter of Robert and Olave Baden-Powell, became President in 1989 and was present at many of the events, four years later, when the Guild celebrated its Golden Jubilee. The same year the Guide Promise was revised and a new logo and design for the Promise badge, to be shared by all members of the Guide Association and the Guild, was introduced. The celebration culminated on 24 November with a tea party attended by the Queen Mother.

4

Modern Girl

Seeing the World

Global guiding is not just about having friends in every corner of the world, but about giving members an opportunity to travel and embrace new experiences. Each year, thousands of Guides travel to the numerous international camps, where members from all over the world meet in such diverse places as Estonia, Korea, New Zealand and the Netherlands.

The Partnership programme encourages contact with Guides in other countries, by twinning units or putting them in touch on a one-off basis. Contact can range from regular emailing or letter-writing to exchange visits, so local Guides can introduce visitors to their country and culture, and then follow it up with a return trip.

The four World Centres owned by the World Association of Girl Guides and Girl Scouts (WAGGGS) have helped provide hundreds of guiding members, and their families, the chance to get together with those from other countries, participate in events and community projects and have a truly unforgettable holiday.

Adventurous Guides can ski in the Swiss Alps, join in a Mexican fiesta, sample the cuisine of India or take in the bright lights of London.

LEFT: Helen Storrow, Falk and Olave Baden-Powell, pictured in 1934

A Swiss family home

The seed for the centres was sown in 1929 when the World Committee decided that an international base, to be shared by all Girl Guides and Girl Scouts, would be a dream come true. The lady who made it into reality was the generous US Girl Scout Leader Helen Storrow, who offered to donate all the funds needed to construct the building and run it for four years, as long as it was built in Switzerland. The Committee accepted and Mrs Storrow, with Swiss leader Ida von Herrenschwand, affectionately known as Falk, set about 'scouting' for locations.

Falk eventually found the perfect spot high up on top of a hill in Adelboden. She and the architect, Mr von Sinner, telegraphed Mrs Storrow, who arrived to climb to the site

LEFT: Our Chalet in the snow

with the World Committee in June 1931. As the ladies tramped up the hill, Mr von Sinner rushed ahead and when the rest of the party reached the top, the American flag was there to greet them. They celebrated with a tea party. By the time Mrs Storrow returned, in May 1932, the Chalet was complete and she asked that a smaller one be built where she could stay and receive her own guests. The Baby Chalet, which still provides accommodation today, was added. Our Chalet, as the main chalet is known, was formally opened by Helen Storrow and Lady Olave Baden-Powell in July 1932, and the indomitable Falk became its first leader. Many gifts from around the world helped to furnish the centre and can still be seen today in the preserved library (or Great Britain Room) and the American Room.

In the Second World War the chalet was closed to the usual visitors but was used, instead, to help reunite refugees and their families. Since reopening, after the war, the building has undergone frequent refurbishments and in 1999 gained a new chalet-style house alongside the main one. The Spycher (the traditional name for a barn in which equipment is stored), provides extra guest accommodation, conference facilities and office space.

A Mexican dream

As they step through the 'Chief's door' visitors to Our Cabaña find themselves in five acres of stunning tropical gardens in the heart of Cuernavaca, the 'city of eternal spring'. Inside the grounds, overlooking the red tiled roofs of the neighbourhood, there are volleyball and tennis courts and a heated swimming pool. Without even leaving the centre guests can soak up Mexican life with a visit to the

RIGHT: Our Cabaña

Our Cabaña song

1. Neath the Grand Sierra Madre on a plain in Mexico,
Lies our beautiful Cabaña, where Girl Scouts and Guides go,
Oh come then to see the mountains, the cactus and sunny skies,
Hear the crickets in the evening and see the white moon arise.

2. En la bella Cuernavaca, en un valle en México,
sencuentra Nuestra Cabaña un lugar lleno de sol,
Vamos a Nuestra Cabaña, gozaremos a llegar
d'amistad y d'alegria y de belleza sin par.

3. When you see the warm red roofs, you think of hearts
 that glow with cheer,
And the walls of sturdy stone work stand for friendship so dear,
Each day there is filled with laughter, each evening is filled with song,
And our stay at Our Cabaña gives us memories life long.

4. Cada día en Nuestra Cabaña, trabajamos por cumplir,
Los ideales de Guidismo y de nuestro fundador,
Vayamos a La Cabaña, nuestra promesa a vivir,
con nuestras hermanas Guías, l'amistad a compartir.

5. When you go to Our Cabaña you will find yourselves at home,
There's a greeting smile so friendly and a handshake so warm.
So come now to Our Cabaña, world friendship to increase,
And carry to our homeland International Peace.

craft house, where traditional arts and crafts are on display, or by dancing to a Mariachi band at a festival.

The idea of a Guide retreat in the Western hemisphere was born on a training session in Cuba in 1946 and was approved by the World Committee six years later. Planners scoured Cuba, Panama and the US for a suitable site before selecting the current plot. The centre opened its doors in 1957 to host the first Juliette Low session, and the Our Cabaña song was penned, to the tune of a traditional Mexican birthday song.

The song was written in alternate Spanish and English verses, to reflect the international nature of the Cabaña. It can sleep up to 90, making it the largest of the World Centres, and its welcoming door saw an astonishing 68,000 visitors pass through in the first 50 years.

An Indian retreat

'Sangam' is a Sanskrit word meaning 'joining together', making it a perfect title for the World Centre in India. When the World Committee was looking to build a centre in the Asia Pacific region, it stipulated that it must be easily accessible by air, bus and train, have a climate which allows its use all year round and should be strongly supported by the local guiding movement.

Bids came in from Australia, Pakistan and the Philippines but, under the determined leadership of Ms Laxmi

LEFT: Guides
can cool off with
a swim in
Sangam's pool

Mazumdar, the National Commissioner of the Bharat Scouts and Guides, it was the Guides in India who won the day. The government of Maharashtra state, in Western India, indicated its own backing by donating nearly eight acres of land near the thriving city of Pune, as well as 100,000 rupees. The close proximity to the culturally rich Pune, as well as being within easy reach of the state capital, Mumbai (then Bombay), made it the perfect location.

The appeal for money brought an overwhelming response from WAGGGS member countries, and Ms Mazumdar personally oversaw the construction of the building,

travelling from New Delhi once a month to check progress. On 16 October 1966, Lady Olave Baden-Powell declared the centre open with the following words:

> 'Love through knowledge and understanding' – this will be carried out in full measure by the young people who will fill this place, and it is with deep joy in my heart that I declare Sangam open.

From the peaceful retreat of Sangam, thousands of Guides and Leaders have explored the local area, or gone further afield on the *Explore India* tour to the Taj Mahal, Jaipur and Delhi.

LEFT: Paxtu, the
Baden-Powells'
home in Kenya

RIGHT: Pax Lodge

BELOW:
Pax Hill, 1925

The world on our doorstep

Although Pax Lodge is the newest of the four World Centres, there has been a World Centre in London since 1939. The first, named Our Ark, was originally next to the World Bureau in Palace Street, where it remained for 20 years. However, housing laws brought in after the Second World War stated that business and residential properties were to be kept completely separate so, when the lease was up in 1959, the Bureau and the World Centre would have had to move. In 1957, to mark the centenary of the Founder's birth, an appeal was launched by Olave Baden-Powell to 'keep the World's heart beating'. On her birthday, she received a gift of actual bricks, inscribed with the amounts collected in each place, which were built into models of the new premises. Two years later the Bureau moved to Ebury Street and Our Ark was relocated in nearby Longridge Road; in 1963 the centre was renamed Olave House, in honour of the World Chief Guide.

Fittingly, the Hon. Betty Clay, daughter of Robert and Olave Baden-Powell, laid the foundation stone of the current World Centre, Pax Lodge, in 1989. A year later the stunning building, in the leafy surroundings of Hampstead, opened its doors to visitors. Built on the site of Rosslyn Lodge, the one-time home of the Earl of Rosslyn, it was renamed to reflect the Baden-Powells' historic links with Pax Hill in Hampshire and Paxtu in Kenya. (Pax is from the Latin, meaning 'peace'.)

Peace sign

In 1990 an international competition held to design a logo for Pax Lodge was won by Australian Alan Rawady. The trefoil represents International Guiding and Girl Scouting, and the dove carrying an olive branch symbolises peace; it is shaped like an ark to reflect the connection with Our Ark.

Pax Hill

Pax Hill, in Hampshire, was the Baden-Powells' family home for over two decades. In 1939 they moved to Kenya, and during the Second World War, the house was commissioned for use by Canadian soldiers. At the end of the war, Olave Baden-Powell donated Pax Hill to the Girl Guide Association to be used as a home craft training centre. The upkeep was financed by interest on the Baden-Powell Memorial Fund until 1953, when the building was sold with Olave's consent. Pax Hill is now a nursing home.

Global Guiding 2

RIGHT: Girls making their Promise in the sea

Wealth of Nations

At the start of the 20th century, when guiding began, the political map of the world was very different from today's, and Britain boasted an extensive 'empire' of foreign territories under its flag. The 1916 Annual Report listed India, Canada, South Africa, Australia, Egypt, Hong Kong, Malay Peninsula, British West Indies and Gibraltar as the Overseas Branches. Census figures from that time show that there were 7,783 Guides in the Overseas Dominions or dependent territories. Over the next 90 years, that figure has grown to two million, although the countries are now split between Commonwealth countries, independent from the UK and with their own Associations, and Branch

LEFT: A carnival in Anguilla promoting guiding

RIGHT: A duck race in the Falklands

BELOW: Brownies in the Falklands

Associations in the dependent territories. In 1916, Leaders in these countries relied on London Headquarters for information and instruction, but slow communication, and the differences in climate, geography and unit sizes, made it impractical to run the organisation in this way. Olave Baden-Powell, seeing the many problems involved, set up the Imperial Council in 1919, which was to include representatives from British East Africa, South Africa, Rhodesia, Uganda, Australia, Canada, Ceylon, Hong Kong, India, Newfoundland, Malaya, Malta, New Zealand, West Indies (Bahamas, Barbados, Bermuda, Jamaica, San Dominica, Trinidad) and North Borneo. The 1921 Annual Report states:

Up to this time news from far away branches of the Girl Guide Movement had only been received spasmodically, and owing to the war and the consequent postal

Census figures in Commonwealth Countries and Branch Associations

(After 1985 those countries still administered by the UK are known as Branch Associations.)

1916   c.10,000 in 8 countries.

1920   25,815 in 28 countries.

1925   70,410 in 35 countries.

1930   115,999 in 45 countries.

1935   170,732 in 39 countries.

1940   193,420 (no number of countries given).

1946   200,480 (no number of countries given).

1950   209,389 (no number of countries given).

1955   358,367 in 52 countries.

1960   495,238 in 54 countries (42 administered by UK and 12 are independent associations).

1965   651,577 in 57 countries (31 administered by UK and 26 are independent associations).

1970   750,322 in 54 countries (30 administered by UK and 24 are independent associations).

1975   670,488 in 53 countries (27 administered by UK and 26 are independent associations).

1980   539,627 (29 countries unable to provide figures). 54 Commonwealth Countries (24 Branch Associations, 30 independent associations).

1985   1,003,524 in 52 Commonwealth Countries (18 Branch Associations, 34 independent associations).

1990   1,317,014 in 55 Commonwealth Countries (11 Branch Associations, 44 independent associations).

1995   1,768,270 (9 Branch Associations and 47 independent associations).

2000   1,810,105 (9 Branch Associations and 42 independent associations).

Source: Census returns

delays there had been very little linking up of Guides throughout the Empire.

On the formation of the Imperial Council, however, Lady Baden-Powell invited ladies to act as corresponding members for the various parts of the Empire where Guides were in existence. These ladies are, wherever possible, connected in some way with the Dominion or Colony with which they correspond, and have therefore special knowledge of the conditions under which the Guides have to work.

As well as opening the lines of communication, the councillors made a special point of contacting Guides who were due to leave the UK to live in a member country, 'and making it easy for them to do guiding wherever they may be going, and also of giving the warmest possible welcome to Guide people from Overseas who are visiting England'. At the first World Camp held at Foxlease in 1924, 300 Guiders from Great Britain and the Dominions took special courses on campers, licences, woodcraft, Brownie and Ranger work. The Chief Guide attended the whole of the camp and Princess Mary hosted lunch on the last day.

During the Second World War Guides in the Imperial countries sent gifts for evacuees and made clothes for the Allied soldiers. Guide Gift Week saw them raise an impressive £12,933.

The 1941 Annual Report said: *Guides in all parts of the Empire are playing their part in the war effort. In some places it is possible for them to do more than others. But whatever may be the job they find to do, they are carrying on faithfully and efficiently, thus according to their opportunities are they contributing finely to the united war effort. Many are the gifts sent home, crates, bales and*

parcels of beautifully made and packed clothes, packages of assorted groceries and sweets; often with most charming greetings from the particular pack or company that sent them tucked in the wrapping, all most useful and most welcome … Most Dominions and Colonies, in addition to sending gifts of clothing and money to England, are supporting their own war charities.

At the beginning of the 1940s, the Branch Associations, which looked after the day-to-day business of the units in each region, numbered 50. As more and more countries became independent of the UK, this reduced to the current number of nine. However, many of the others, who now had their own Associations, maintained close ties with the UK under the umbrella of the Commonwealth, administered from Commonwealth Headquarters in London.

The importance of the Commonwealth countries is demonstrated by the Commonwealth Conference, held every three years between 1960 and 1981 at Foxlease, with the exception of the 1972 meeting, which took place in Jamaica. Since 1981 it has been held in numerous Commonwealth cities including Toronto, Kuala Lumpur, Singapore and Malta. The most recent conference was held in Cape Town in July 2008 and was followed by a two-day meeting of Branch Association members.

In March 1971 Chief Commissioner Ann Parker Bowles arrived in Canada at the start of her Commonwealth tour, which lasted several weeks and covered 42,000 miles. From Canada she flew to New Zealand, visiting every state, then on to Tasmania and Papua New Guinea. At each stop, she found guiding was thriving in the area.

Branching out

Branch Associations look after guiding members who live in UK Overseas Territories – countries which have chosen to maintain political links with the UK and still have the Queen as their head of state. There are currently nine Branch members: Montserrat, the British Virgin Islands, Anguilla,

A friend in need

Montserrat is a small volcanic island in the Caribbean Sea which, until 1995, had a population of 12,000. In that year, volcanic eruptions from Mount Soufrière caused a great many families to flee the island and many more to move to temporary accommodation in the north. A catastrophic eruption in 1997 destroyed houses and businesses, closed airports and seaports and caused yet more to flee.

The eruption also destroyed the Guide Headquarters, which had been open less than ten years. As always, members elsewhere reached out a helping hand, and in 2007 rebuilding work began using money raised by the Guides and Brownies of north-east England.

Bermuda, the Cayman Islands, the Falklands, Gibraltar, St Helena and Turks and Caicos.

Guides in these territories make the same Promise as those in the UK and wear the same uniform, although the hotter regions choose the more lightweight options. On the whole, they follow the same programme, although minor adjustments are made to take climate and economic conditions into consideration. For example, Guides and Brownies in the Caribbean can earn a Caribbean Knowledge badge, and camps are usually held indoors since the lack of shade makes camping with tents impossible. Each region has its own President and Council, though support is given from the UK, and the Chief Guide is also the head of the Branch Associations.

UK international camps, such as the one in Foxlease in 1999, give the Branch Association members a chance to meet their UK counterparts and members from the other territories, and the Associations are often represented at major events, such as the Queen's Coronation in 1953, when five Guides from Gibraltar attended the ceremony.

Going for GOLD 2

Anne Young and Amelia Sutcliffe set off for Madagascar in 2007 as team members of a five-year project. Their task was to teach English, at beginner, intermediate and advance levels, and to assist in the areas of arts and crafts, leadership and self-esteem, women's rights and problem solving.

BELOW: The GOLD team in Madagascar in 2007

Anne Young explained:

We worked with both village children and Guides and Guiders in Madagascar and all this was made possible by the group of Mpanazava Guides that formed part of our team. These guides acted as our fellow planners, translators and – especially – friends. It was fantastic to get to know them and work with them – it allowed us a real insight into the lives of young Madagascan women, who were all trying to make a difference in both their own and others' lives.

Working in the villages could be a bit manic at times but was a thrilling experience and I hope that in our short time there we managed to both teach the children and also give them a couple of days of fun away from their normal activities. Also, we were lucky enough to visit a couple of different rainforests and see some of the famous lemurs, only found in Madagascar. This was such a special experience. The country's Minister for the Environment was very generous and helped us out more than we could have ever expected with our journeys.

Being invited to be part of a GOLD project was an absolute honour and is something that I will always hold close to my heart. The people I met and the experiences I had created a fantastic and very original four weeks for me. I look forward to returning to Madagascar in years to come and seeing what progress has been made in the general well-being of the country. The girls I went on project with are still all in contact and we regularly meet to catch up on each other's lives. Only we share those experiences and I feel very lucky to have been part of that.

Amelia Sutcliffe agrees:

Madagascar was absolutely fantastic ... It's a very poor country but they are very generous – anything they've got they'll give you. The Guides were exactly like Guides in this country, except for the language, so that was really strange. When we got there we had a chat about boys and they were all going on about the boys from school, and I was surprised how similar they were in their attitudes to the girls over here. They were just typical teenagers. Before I signed up to go to Madagascar I'd never even been to London before and we had our briefing meetings there, so I had to get a train down and go on a tube. I'd only been on package holidays to Europe and, this time, I had to travel with near strangers, people I'd only met two or three times – but it gave me a lot of confidence. I'm training to be a teacher now and it really helped me in thinking about different backgrounds. I find that I talk a lot about Madagascar while I'm teaching, and the situation they have over there, and my girls really respond to it. I was already heavily involved with guiding but this made me realise how fantastic the organisation is. We seemed to have an instant bond with the Madagascan people and that came about through guiding. It's all on such a massive scale and I had never thought about it in those terms before.

BELOW: Harriet Taylor
with Thai Guides

Harriet Taylor's GOLD experience took her to Thailand, where she and seven others ran workshops on various topics including self-esteem, positive women, mental health, leadership and being healthy.

My commitment to GOLD 2007 began in December 2005 when I was selected for the Thailand project along with three other members of Girlguiding UK. We prepared during four briefing weekends and through telephone conferences. On arrival in Thailand we met with four members of Guiding Australia. Our team of eight were aged between 18 and 30, with varying degrees of guiding and travel experience, and all very excited to have been chosen and to be representing our countries.

In Thailand, guiding is a school subject. Pupils have the choice of Girl Guides, Scouts or the Red Cross, and lessons take place once a week with around 200 girls in a class – they sit at desks and learn guiding principles. Our GOLD project aimed to develop the Thai Association and provide workshops. We wanted to show both Leaders and girls what guiding could be and to stimulate new ideas for lesson activities.

Our workshops were delivered to around 150 members of the Girl Guide Association of Thailand with three-day camps just outside Bangkok and near Chiang Mai in the north. My subjects were leadership, for adults, and being healthy for the girls. In the leadership session I shared ideas on a variety of activities for the teachers to use with their Guides and also on planning the lessons. Girls took part in activities based on healthy eating and exercise, and avoiding drugs, smoking and alcohol. One of my great highlights of the trip was to see the smiles

ABOVE: GOLD project in South Africa 2007

and laughter as groups participated and enjoyed the experience. Our trip was not all work though, as our hosts were keen to share their country with us. We enjoyed visiting tourist sights in Bangkok and Chiang Mai, as well as spending a night with a northern hill tribe. We were privileged to participate in the 50th Anniversary Celebrations of the Girl Guide Association of Thailand.

As a GOLD team we also took part in evening activities at the camps, sharing UK and Australian culture and organising campfires. My involvement in the project brought much personal benefit for me – my personal confidence developed, in delivering workshops and training, and especially in exploring and discussing new subjects. I brought many ideas back to UK, in particular Australian and Thai activities to pass on to my Guides and other members of Girlguiding UK. The fascination of local Guides and Brownies when I shared ideas and stories has been amazing, and I hope this will encourage them to explore international opportunities in the future.

Changing the World

Girlguiding UK: Changing the world

Commemorating an event as special as Girlguiding UK's Centenary has, in true guiding style, called for a challenge.

In a project named 'Changing the World', Girlguiding UK joined forces with 18 well-known charities and its own Branch Associations to come up with 19 ways for the girls to make a real difference to today's world by contributing time, raising funds or giving voice to a cause. As Chief Guide Liz Burnley explains, 'It's a project that's bringing us all together in the run-up to the Centenary, which is really exciting, and follows exactly the kinds of actions the girls have been taking for 100 years.' Projects range from tree-planting for the Woodland Trust and anti-bullying workshops to sending books to poor countries and helping to build a school in Liberia.

Liz Burnley is excited about the way ahead for the ever-enthusiastic Guides:

Changing the World – a fairly modest aspiration! There has always been a tradition of being of service to others and playing a role in your community and in society, and that has meant different things at different times. The Guide International Service, for example, saw women doing amazing heroic things for the war effort, which was needed at that time. The message we are putting out today is that little things make a big difference. If you add up a lot of little actions, it doesn't take much for that to become something really big.

And because we have a tradition of always being linked to the community that we're part of, we have always been well placed to make things happen. Changing the World is a brilliant way of showing people in a focused way, both for us internally and externally, what is possible, and the idea is that girls will find out about something – an issue, a charity or cause – that they didn't know much about. Perhaps they will try some activities, to make it fun to find out about the issue, and they'll think about what they might do in terms of advocacy for the issue or raising funds for a charity.

Indeed, Girl Guides have been changing the world in many different ways since 1910, from visiting the elderly and sick on a local level, to raising funds for global and environmental projects.

The things I've learned make me think and care more about the world.
Jorgia, 80th Newcastle-upon-Tyne (Holy Cross) Guides

THIS PAGE: Girls taking part in Changing the World Activities

Adopt and Cherish

In 1981 the Guides joined forces with the Keep Britain Tidy Group and Lloyds Bank to launch Adopt and Cherish. Each girl adopted a piece of land to look after, and took responsibility for its upkeep.

The scheme lasted three years and won the Queen Mother's 80th Birthday Award. In addition, an exhibition was mounted at the Houses of Parliament in 1983.

RIGHT:
Girls muck in as they clear a river for the Adopt and Cherish project in 1982

FAR RIGHT:
Adopt and Cherish Poster

BOTTOM RIGHT:
Adopt and Cherish project, 1982

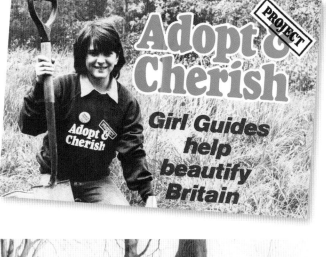

PRIMARY HEALTH CARE
PROJECT
SRI LANKA 1985

LEFT: Publicity
material for the
Primary Health
Care project,
Sri Lanka

BOTTOM:
Sri Lanka
project badge

I'm helping UNICEF in Sri Lanka

Helping Sri Lanka's children

To celebrate the 75th anniversary of guiding, in 1985 a Primary Health Care project was set up in conjunction with UNICEF. As it was the International Year of Youth, the project was to provide immunisation for children in Sri Lanka. The original plan was for a year-long project to raise £25,000, but the response was so overwhelming that guiding members continued to provide aid to the country for several years afterwards. In August 1985 a group of Rangers and Venture Scouts went out to Sri Lanka to build wells and lavatory blocks, improving sanitation in the poor villages. In 1988 the Guides took action to fight childhood disease by throwing their fundraising weight behind Polioplus, a campaign run by the Rotary Club, which aimed to end polio and control five other killer diseases.

Saving the environment

Recycling may be the buzzword of the 21st century but the Guides have been doing it for 100 years! The principle of thrift, instilled in Guides from day one, encourages girls to mend, sew or reuse – anything rather than throw things away. Lord Baden-Powell himself took the principle to extraordinary lengths, and would save notepaper by writing replies to the letters he received in the margin and sending them back.

In 1918, while the First World War still raged in Europe, the National Salvage Company asked the Guides to collect fruit stones and nutshells as a matter of urgency, and send them to the Southend Gas Works. As each parcel arrived, a new label was sent out for the next consignment, and the girls happily did their duty without having a clue what the stones and shells were being used for. Finally the curator of the Gas Museum discovered the secret – they contained potash, which it was believed could absorb poison gas, so they were being ground down for use in gas masks.

The girls also collected horse chestnuts for munitions factories and herbs for hospitals and dispensaries. Foil milk-bottle tops and cigarette wrappers were saved to help the war effort and the Leaders asked girls to gather up cigar tubes and the insides of fountain pens to send to scrap-metal merchants.

There were even greater efforts in the Second World War, with the Guides collecting anything and everything, from empty jam jars and rags to used razor blades and batteries. Since then, recycling has featured in the guiding programme daily, with special projects including the collection of aluminium cans for Alcan, and the recycling of ink cartridges and mobile phones.

The Environmental Challenge

Cold winter winds do not stop Girl Guides thinking about global warming. In 1998 they wrapped themselves up and got digging for the Environmental Challenge. Launched by David Bellamy at the Natural History Museum, the project aimed to cut carbon dioxide emissions and plant as many trees as possible. Thousands of girls responded to the call and, over the next year and a half, managed to collect over a million cans, plant over 300,000 trees and help cut carbon dioxide emissions by a huge amount.

RIGHT: Environment Challenge badge

LEFT: Collecting fir cones for fuel in 1940

RIGHT: Girls join Philippa Forrester and David Bellamy to launch the Environmental Challenge

Making a splash

Six years of aquatic fun for girls around Britain meant life-saving water supplies for thousands of people in Africa and Asia. Between 1993 and 1998 Wacky Washes took place all over the country, and an average of £15,000 was raised each year. Activities ranged from washing an Air UK jet to holding water Olympics and water quizzes. Some of the more imaginative ideas were rewarded with a free day out at Alton Towers and, before the trip, the girls even washed the coaches taking them there – in return for cut-price travel of course!

RIGHT: Brownies washed Flossy the Elephant at Dudley Zoo during the Week of Water Wacky Wash, 1995

Some of the Changing the World projects

The Changing the World initiative got off to a great start. The 1st Witnesham Brownies decided to take part in the World Wildlife Fund-UK One Planet project, raising awareness of environmental issues.

We spent a great deal of time discussing our rubbish, how we could cut down and help produce less damage to our environment by making full use of recycling. The girls answered questions about how we can make a difference by buying food with less packaging and making sure we recycle everything possible.

Posters were created to encourage others to think about recycling. The Brownies were presented with a variety of everyday consumables and everyone, including Leaders, was really shocked at how far the items travel before coming into our homes! We discussed the impact on the environment that buying items made in other countries can have.

With two weeks of rubbish collected, the Brownies created a rubbish monster sculpture made from plastic, cardboard and newspaper, and a band was formed using instruments made from recycled products.

The 116th Bristol (Bishopsworth) Guide company learned about living on the streets with runaways' charity The Railway Children.

We were very shocked to find out that so many children run away from home and that lots of these children are only the same age as us. We discussed why people run away and what we should do so that we never get into this position.

We made a shelter from canes and black bags and lined it out with newspapers just to see what it was like to live on the street. We made dream catchers and talked about the dreams of some of the children in the pack – we realised that their dreams are very similar to ours, even though we come from happy homes and lives.

As a fundraiser we did a sponsored sleep in a cardboard box. We spent the night in our boxes and we raised £186.

The 1st South Bath Rainbows and 24th Bath Brownies picked the National Deaf Children's Society Hands Up project, which encourages children to learn sign language, because one of their Young Leaders is partially deaf.

We decided to jointly support this project. The Rainbows and Brownies have been learning how to make their Promise in sign language and have taken part in a number of activities relating to deafness-promoting awareness. The girls really threw themselves into the activities and all came out with a new appreciation of what it must like to be deaf.

RIGHT: Recycling cards for the Woodland Trust

BOTTOM LEFT: Hosting an island café for the Branch Associations

BOTTOM RIGHT: Guides 'Adopt-a-shop' for Save the Children

The 53rd Hull Guides learned about AIDS and HIV awareness for UNICEF's Say Yes project.

We held several games to make the girls aware of HIV and AIDS, and produced posters, leaflets and cards to display around our local church as well as taking them home. Girls were encouraged to talk about people who were affected by HIV and AIDS – not just those infected but all their family and the knock-on effect it has.

The youngest members reached out to help the old and ill when 1st Lothersdale Rainbows chose the Live, Love, Let Go project for Help the Hospices.

We have held a coffee morning to raise money, painted swirly snakes to hang up in the local hospice and coloured in pictures to decorate the TV room. The local hospice funding team is visiting us to tell us more about hospices.

LEFT:
Girls plant
trees for the
Woodland Trust

Trains, Planes and Lifeboats

A brave Brownie earned a shilling by having a tooth out without crying, a Guide polished boots at a police station and another gave skating lessons to three young men – small but significant actions and many more like them added up to a remarkable gift to help the war effort in 1940.

The appeal was Guide Gift Week, when older members were asked to give up half a day's salary to buy two air ambulances for the RAF, and younger girls were asked to give up pocket money or raise cash any way they could. Girls set about weeding gardens, helping with furniture removal, painting gateposts and kerbs white so they were less of a danger in the blackout, mending clothes and babysitting. One Scottish lass taught English phrases to an African student for a small fee. Chief Commissioner Mrs St John Atkinson had asked for £20,000 with the cry 'Can we do it …? Of course we can!' and a week of frenzied activities proved that not only could they do it, they could double it.

A terrific total of £50,296 was raised and the badly needed aeroplanes, specially fitted to ferry wounded soldiers from the front in France, were bought. The remaining money was used to buy 20 motor ambulances, which were presented to the Royal Navy, and one very special lifeboat.

RIGHT: Guides presenting 20 motor ambulances to the Navy in 1940

FAR RIGHT: Brownies and Guides had a good look inside the air ambulance after the presentation in 1940

Dunkirk spirit

Since 1939 a lifeboat had been under construction in the Rowhedge yard on the River Colne in Essex. It was due to go into service on the coast of Cornwall, but had not yet been paid for. When the call came for all small craft available to rescue the soldiers of the British Army trapped on the beaches of Dunkirk in France, the new lifeboat sprang into action. She travelled back and forth across the Channel, ferrying exhausted and wounded men to safety, at great cost to her new wood and smart paintwork. Machine-gun bullets and shrapnel pierced and buffeted her sides. The engine was badly damaged, a rope got tangled in the propeller and the foresail was ripped, yet she limped home somehow.

The Guides donated £5,000 to the Royal National Lifeboat Institution, which used the money to buy the boat, after all the repairs. The heroic little vessel, renamed the *Guide of Dunkirk*, went on to serve Cadgwith Lifeboat Station on the Cornish coast, saving 17 lives before being retired and sold to John Moor of Mevagissey, whose family served in the lifeboat crew. Under a new name, *Girl Guide*, she was used for pleasure and fishing trips and in 1983 was adopted by the Dunkirk Veterans Association.

RIGHT: The *Guide of Dunkirk*

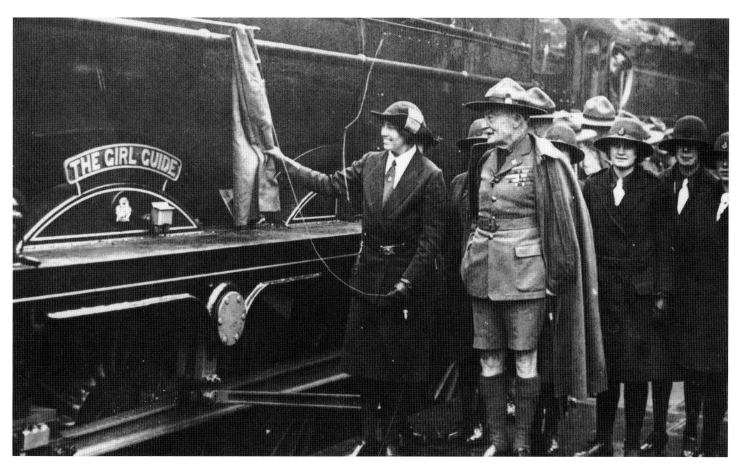

Full speed ahead

The girls of the 4th Derby (LMS) Troop put their engineering skills to work in 1930 by helping to build a train in a single week! Engines 6168 and 6169, renamed *The Girl Guide* and *The Boy Scout*, were the last of a batch of 20 Royal Scot class designed by the London, Midland and Scottish Railway Chief Mechanical Engineer, Sir Henry Fowler, an ex-Scout Commissioner.

On 9 December 12 Guides and four Scouts made up the guard of honour at a special presentation by Lord Robert and Lady Olave Baden-Powell at Euston Station. Plates with the Trefoil and Fleur de Lis badge were fixed to the engines as they stood at platform 6, ready to take their places as the most powerful express engines in use between Euston and Scotland.

After 16 years as a passenger train *The Girl Guide* was adapted for freight work between Crewe and the West. In 1966 she was finally taken out of service and her engine plate was presented to the Association and is now in the archives.

The Future Beckons

The Chief Guide, Liz Burnley, shares her vision for the future of guiding for the next 100 years.

I've been involved in guiding ever since I was seven, and joined as a Brownie. In many ways guiding hasn't changed, in terms of the basics, and what we're about. For me the thing that has changed is the look and the feel of it, because time moves on. The uniforms are much more funky and nowadays there's a choice. The programme I followed was really relevant when I was a Brownie, but that's different from what's relevant today, so while the core values remain the same, the detail of it has more than kept pace.

At certain times in our history we've moved on quicker than others and in recent years technology has made a huge difference. When I see the photograph of the girls at the Crystal Palace Rally in 1909, I look at those faces and wonder 'What was life like for them?' This was before two world wars, before women even had the vote – it was a very different age and a hugely different context. It's really wonderful to think about what those girls were doing. It would have been very courageous in those times to say, 'We're girls, but we want a piece of this action as well.' It's inspirational and I like to think we can still capture that spirit today. For me, that photo is quite iconic and it's incredibly interesting to look back at our beginnings and see just how

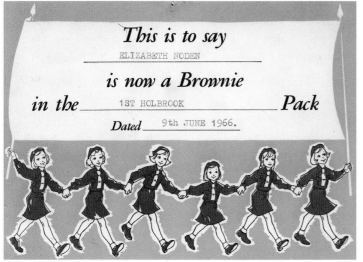

This is to say

ELIZABETH NODEN

is now a Brownie

in the ___1ST HOLBROOK___ Pack

Dated ___9th JUNE 1966.___

ABOVE: *I still have my certificate from when I became a member of the 1st Holbrook Brownie Pack. I was very proud of that and still am. The rusty mark is from the drawing pin which stuck it on to my notice board for many years!*

LEFT: Liz (2nd from left) with inspirational Leader Rita Aris at Queen's Guide Service

RIGHT: Liz with Rainbows in 2006

groundbreaking guiding was. Our challenge for the next century is to keep the spirit alive and help it grow in a way that works for new times.

Guiding is a global family and our sister organisations around the world are dealing with a phenomenal number of issues in their own particular countries. In South Africa they're tackling AIDS awareness, in Kenya it's the issue of female genital mutilation. I myself went to visit a women's prison in Pakistan, a really tough environment, but the Guides were in there teaching literacy skills.

I believe guiding is more relevant today than ever, because life is changing very fast for girls and young women, and because we are the largest organisation for girls and young women we've got the chance to help them to shout out on issues they care about. They don't often have that opportunity in other areas of their lives and they don't have a female-only space. We continually ask our members what they think about being in a girl-only environment and their answer, consistently, is that it makes a real difference

because they can be themselves without external pressure, they can learn about leadership and take up roles – and they can be daft and have fun – in a way they can't in a mixed environment. Our research shows that girls and young women feel under a lot of pressure today in terms of bullying, body image and health issues, and we're actually a safe space that isn't school, where they can form a different set of relationships through guiding.

Ahead of us is a huge opportunity to make sure that what we offer continues to be really relevant and driven by the girls themselves. I think the more we do to ask them what they want, what they care about and how they want things to operate, and the more we involve them in leading us forward, the better chance we have of being relevant in the future. It's not me who knows what the right programme activity might be for a seven-year-old – she's got views herself on what kinds of things would be interesting, what she will learn from and grow from. So one of our biggest challenges is to really make sure that we are led by our members.

The Centenary is a wonderful point to pause and celebrate what we've achieved as an organisation. Since those first girls in 1909, a staggering number of women have been members at some stage in their lives. If you add them all up over 100 years, it's a huge body of people and the fact that the amazing dedication of our volunteers has had a positive effect on so many should be celebrated. I also see the Centenary as the start of the next 100 years, and it's a very exciting opportunity to look at how we move forward, how we remember our roots and our traditions and take up the challenge of where that should lead in the future.

Guiding gives you confidence in today's world – it helps you to be individual and your own person rather than following the crowd.
Emma, 2nd Liversedge Guides

Key Dates in Guiding

1907 Robert Baden-Powell holds a camp for boys at Brownsea Island.

1908 *Scouting for Boys* by Baden-Powell is published, and girls as well as boys begin Scouting.

1909 Girls calling themselves Girl Scouts attend the first Boy Scout Rally at Crystal Palace, and attract the attention of Baden-Powell, who realises that a scheme for girls must be thought out.

1910 Agnes Baden-Powell, sister of Robert Baden-Powell, takes responsibility for girls wishing to continue Scouting, and the Girl Guides Association is formed.

1912 Robert Baden-Powell marries Olave Soames, who soon exercises a powerful and beneficial influence on the young Girl Guide movement.

The first Guide handbook, called *How Girls Can Help Build up the Empire,* is published.

1914 A junior section, called 'Rosebuds', for girls under 11 is formed (renamed Brownies in 1915).

1916 Senior Guide groups formed (renamed 'Rangers' in 1920).

Olave Baden-Powell (later GBE) appointed the first Chief Commissioner.

1918 Olave Baden-Powell appointed Chief Guide.

1919 The International Council (the forerunner of the World Association of Girl Guides and Girl Scouts, WAGGGS) is formed.

1920 HRH The Princess Mary becomes President of the Association.

The first International Conference is held at Oxford.

1922 The Association is granted a Royal Charter of Incorporation.

The first Guide Training Centre is opened in Hampshire (Foxlease).

1924 First World Camp takes place at Foxlease.

1926 Thinking Day is instituted (22 February, the joint birthdays of Olave and Robert Baden-Powell, is chosen as the day on which all members of the movement give special thought to the worldwide fellowship of guiding).

Lady Delia Peel (later DCVO) appointed Chief Commissioner.

1928 The World Association of Girl Guides and Girl Scouts (WAGGGS) is formed.

1930 Olave Baden-Powell is acclaimed World Chief Guide.

Mrs Mary Birley (JP, later CBE) appointed Chief Commissioner.

1931 Queen Mary opens the new Guide Headquarters at Buckingham Palace Road.

1932 Coming-of-age celebrations for the Association's 21st birthday (postponed from 1931 because of the national economic crisis) take place.

The First World Guide Centre is opened in Switzerland (Our Chalet).

1937 The Princesses Elizabeth and Margaret enrol as a Guide and Brownie respectively.

Queen Elizabeth (later the Queen Mother) becomes Patron of the Association.

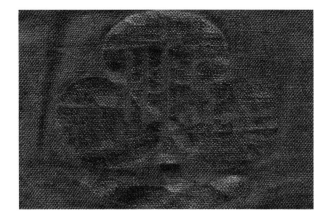

1939 Mrs Lorna St John Atkinson appointed Chief Commissioner.

1940 Guide Gift Week: Guides of the Commonwealth raise over £50,000 to help the war effort, by giving up half a day's salary, forfeiting pocket money, or by earning it in a variety of ways.

Home Emergency Scheme to equip Rangers for National Service is introduced.

1941 Robert Baden-Powell dies at the age of 83.

1942 Guide International Service (GIS) Committee set up to select and train Guiders for relief work after the war.

Lady Finola Somers CBE appointed Chief Commissioner.

1943 The Trefoil Guild is formed for members of the movement over the age of 21 who wish to keep in touch with guiding but are unable to undertake regular work with Guides.

1946 The Queens Guide Badge is instituted as the highest testwork achievement for Guides.

1949 The Lady Jean Strathenden and Campbell CBE appointed Chief Commissioner.

1953 Coronation Year: Guides throughout the Commonwealth undertake projects as their Tribute of Service to make the Queen's realm more beautiful.

HM The Queen becomes Joint Patron with Queen Elizabeth (the Queen Mother).

1956 Miss Anstice Gibbs (later DCVO, CBE) appointed Chief Commissioner.

1957 Centenary year: Guides celebrate the birth of Baden-Powell in 1857; world camps are held in Windsor, Switzerland, Canada and the Philippines.

1959 Rangers are among the first girls to gain the Duke of Edinburgh's award. (Rangers helped to pilot the scheme).

1960 Golden Jubilee of the Association: Guides celebrate by undertaking service projects linked with World Refugee Year.

1964 The Guide Friendship Fund is initiated. Its aim is to enable Guides to help worthy projects overseas, mainly in the Commonwealth, and to support a few national ones each year, besides giving immediate aid in cases of disaster.

1965 Princess Margaret becomes President of the Association, following the death of Princess Mary.

1966 Guides break the girls' relay record, swimming the English Channel.

Mrs Ann Parker Bowles (later DCVO, CBE) becomes Chief Commissioner.

1968 New programme for all sections, giving them greater unity, freedom and flexibility, comes into being.

1970 Diamond Jubilee of the Association: Guides celebrate with the theme 'Three Cheers' and give service by cheering a person, a place and themselves.

1973 Link (a branch of the Girl Guides Association for former Rangers and Venture Scouts aged 18–30 who, together with their friends, wish to give practical service to the Scout and Guide movements) is formed.

The Young Leader's Scheme starts for girls aged 16–18 who wish to work with Brownies and Guides. They do not have to have been in the Guide movement before to join the scheme.

1975 Mrs Sheila Walker JP (later CBE) becomes Chief Commissioner.

1977 Olave Baden-Powell dies at the age of 88.

1979 The first Olave Baden-Powell bursaries are given to Guides and Rangers to help broaden their experience or develop a skill.

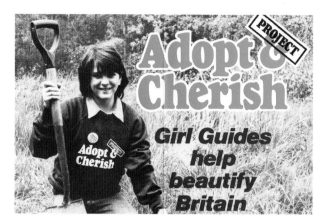

International Year of the Child: all sections of the Guide movement are encouraged to find out about children in other countries and their own, whose way of life, environment and circumstances differ from theirs.

1980 Junior Council of the Association (renamed Innovate) comes into being for those aged 16–26, giving them the opportunity to participate more fully in the affairs of the Association, by providing a forum for debate on national issues, and on those of concern.

Lady Patience Baden-Powell (later CBE) becomes Chief Commissioner.

1981 Joint memorial stone to Olave and Robert Baden-Powell dedicated in Westminster Abbey.

International Year of the Disabled: all sections of the movement are challenged to think about the difficulties of mobility for the disabled and the difficulty of access to buildings, particularly Girl Guide ones.

'Adopt and Cherish' is initiated, a successful conservation campaign that encourages Brownies, Guides and Rangers to become more aware of their environment.

1982 Stamp featuring guiding issued by the British Post Office.

1983 Changes in the Guide and Ranger programmes.

1984 Women into Science and Engineering Year (WISE'84): the Girl Guide Association devises challenges for Brownies, Guides and Rangers on this theme.

The Trefoil Guild extends its membership to men.

1985 The 75th anniversary of the Association.

Dr June Paterson Brown (later CBE) becomes Chief Commissioner.

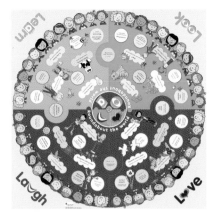

1987 Rainbows, a new section for 5–7-year-olds, is introduced.

1989 The 100th anniversary of the birth of Olave Baden-Powell.

Brownies celebrate their 75th anniversary.

1990 The new uniform, designed by Jeff Banks, is introduced.

90th birthday of the Association.

Mrs Jane Garside JP (later CBE) becomes Chief Commissioner.

1991 75th anniversary of the Ranger Section.

1994 The Girl Guides Association is renamed The Guide Association.

The wording of both the Promise and the Law are changed.

1995 Mrs Margaret Wright (later MBE) becomes Chief Commissioner.

1996 Miss Bridget Towle (later CBE) becomes Chief Guide (name changed from Chief Commissioner).

1997 The 10th birthday of Rainbows is celebrated.

2001 Mrs Jenny Leach (later CBE) becomes Chief Guide.

2002 The Guide Association is rebranded Girlguiding UK.

2003 HRH The Countess of Wessex, becomes Girlguiding UK President.

2004 Brownies celebrate their 90th birthday.

2006 Senior Section mark their 90th birthday.

Mrs Liz Burnley becomes Chief Guide.

2008 Rainbows' 21st birthday.

Picture Credits

All images are credited to Girlguiding UK except for the following.

Introduction

Title page Laura Ashman, p. 2 top left Rob Johnston, p. 2 top right Tanya Lloyd, p. 2 bottom right Laura Ashman, p. 2 bottom left Niall Hartley

Something for Everyone

p. 4 Laura Ashman, p. 10 The Scout Association, p. 12 courtesy of WAGGGS, p. 13 both Niall Hartley, p. 15 courtesy of WAGGGS, p. 18 both Niall Hartley, p. 19 Lady Alport, p. 20 courtesy of WAGGGS, p. 21 courtesy of WAGGGS, p. 22 courtesy of Girl Scouts of America, p. 23 courtesy of Girl Scouts of America, p. 24 left Niall Hartley, p. 25 left Laura Ashman, p. 29 right Northern Army Group, Germany [PR Section], p. 31 Niall Hartley, p. 33 John Leng, p. 34 right 2nd Abbey Rainbows, p. 35 Jack Fisher, p. 36 John Leng, p. 40 Julie Larner, p. 41 Rob Johnston, p. 43 Central Press Photos, p. 44 Studio Lisa, p. 45 left Studio Lisa, p. 45 right Kemsley & Graphic, p. 46 right Thompson Picture Services, p. 49 left London Picture Services, p.50 Henry Iddon, p. 51 Laura Ashman, p. 52 left Mendoza Galleries, p. 55 left Lutterworth Press, p. 55 right Kenneth Brookes, p. 56 Daily Express, p. 58 Millicent Sowerby, p. 59 far left The Medici Society, p. 60 left Sarah Hole

A Guiding Voice

p. 62 Rob Johnston, p. 64 Tanya Lloyd, p. 66 bottom left Laura Ashman, p. 66 bottom right Richard Bailey, p. 67 Laura Ashman, p. 68 Laura Ashman, p. 69 Laura Ashman, p. 70 Fox Photos, p. 73 Imperial War Museum, p. 79 Daily Mirror, p. 81 Fox Photos, p. 82 Allied Newspapers Manchester, p. 83 Fox Photos, p. 84 Kemsley and Graphic, p. 85 right Bournemouth Evening Echo, p. 87 left Illustrated News, p. 91 Keystone, p. 93 right Laura Ashman, p. 95 left and top centre courtesy of Dame Tanni Grey-Thompson and Critical Tortoise, p. 95 bottom centre and right courtesy of Diana Moran, p. 96 Chris Davies/ArenaPAL/ TopFoto, p. 97 left JoJo Maman Bébé Limited, p. 97 right National Pictures/ TopFoto, p. 98 TopFoto/UPP, p. 99 left Laura Ashman, p. 99 top right Rob Johnston, p. 99 bottom right Kate Durrant, p. 104 London Express News, p. 106 courtesy of Salmiya Brownies, p. 110 right courtesy of 1st Muscat Senior Section

Girl Power

p. 112 Richard Bailey, p. 114 Central Press Photos, p. 115 United Press International (UK), p. 121 Niall Hartley, p. 122 all Niall Hartley, p. 123 courtesy of Jubilee Sailing Trust, p. 125 Rob Johnston, p. 126 Niall Hartley, p. 127 left Katrin Ribbe, p. 127 right Niall Hartley, p. 128 Rob Johnston, p. 129 top Laura Ashman, p. 129 bottom Henry Iddon, p. 130 both Abigail Latter, p. 132 Niall Hartley, p. 133 both Niall Hartley, p. 134 Niall Hartley, p. 135 Niall Hartley, p. 136 Jane Eaton, p. 137 right Jane Eaton, p. 139 left Laura Ashman, p. 140 left courtesy of Ally Capellino, p. 140 centre Rob Johnston, p. 140 right Tanya Lloyd, p. 141 Otto Brown, p. 143 Harry Hammond, p. 144 Lancashire Evening Post, p. 145 right Rob Johnston, p. 147 Tanya Lloyd, p. 153 Barratts Photo Press Ltd, p. 155 Niall Hartley, p. 157 Miss Harbon, p. 159 left Jane Eaton, p. 159 right Rob Johnston, p. 161 Laura Ashman, p. 162 Richard Bailey, p. 163 top Laura Ashman, p. 163 bottom Rosie Greaves, p. 164 Fox Photos, p. 166 The Associated Press, p. 167 Laura Ashman, p. 168 Rob Johnston, p. 169 Niall Hartley

Modern Girl

p. 170 Niall Hartley, p. 173 courtesy of WAGGGS, p. 174 courtesy of WAGGGS, p. 175 courtesy of WAGGGS, p. 177 courtesy of WAGGGS, p. 178 top left and top right courtesy of WAGGGS, p. 186 courtesy of Amelia Sutcliffe, p. 187 courtesy of Pauline Henry, p. 188 courtesy of Harriet Taylor, p. 191 top left Rachel Bates, p. 191 top right Janet Butler, p. 191 bottom right Kathryn Phillips, p. 191 bottom left Jacquey Thurlow, p. 192 left and bottom Echo Basildon, p. 195 Strobe Communications, p. 196 Caters Photographic, p. 197 Gemma Smith, p. 198 top Tina Honeysett, p. 198 left Lyn Ford, p. 198 right Kathryn Phillips, p. 199 Gemma Smith, p. 200 Central Press Photos, p. 201 Topical Press, p. 202 RNLI, p. 204 both Laura Ashman, p. 205 Laura Ashman, p. 206 Niall Hartley, p. 207 top left Laura Ashman, p. 207 top right Laura Ashman, p. 207 bottom Jane Eaton, p. 211 left United Press International (UK)

Acknowledgements

With many thanks to Margaret Courtney for her boundless knowledge and generous help. Thanks, too, to Abigail Latter and Karen Taylor for their research and to Jenny Leach, Claire Rees, Nithya Rae and Jessica Peters for their time.

Finally, my gratitude goes to Marjorie Seal and Ann Ferguson, once my own Guiders and a great source of information for the book, as well as all those involved in Guiding who spared their time and their knowledge.

Bibliography

Barne, Kitty, *Here Come the Girl Guides*, London: The Girl Guides Association, 1946

Christian, Catherine, *The Big Test: The Story of the Girl Guides in the World War*, London: The Girl Guides Association, 1947

Forbes, Cynthia (ed.), *The Girl Guide Album*, London: The Girl Guides Association, 1984

Kerr, Rose, *Story of the Girl Guides (1908–1938)*, London: The Girl Guides Association, 1932

Liddell, Alix, *Story of the Girl Guides (1938-1975)*, London: The Girl Guides Association, 1976

Synge, V.M., *Royal Guides: A Story of the 1st Buckingham Place Company*, London: The Girl Guides Association, 1948

Thompson, Vronwyn M., *1910 and Then: A Brief History of the Girl Guides Association*, London: The Girl Guides Association, 1990

If you were involved in guiding in the past, visit www.girlguiding.org.uk to find out about our website aimed at putting past members in touch with each other.

Index